Training with the Heart Rate Monitor

Training with the Heart Rate Monitor

Kuno Hottenrott

Meyer & Meyer Sport

Original Title: Trainingskontrolle mit Herzfrequenz-Messgeräten
© Meyer & Meyer Verlag, 2006
Translated by Heather Ross

British Library Cataloguing in Publication Data
A catalogue record for this book is available from the British Library

Kuno Hottenrott
Training with the Heart Rate Monitor
Oxford: Meyer & Meyer Sport (UK) Ltd., 2007
ISBN: 978-1-84126-213-0

© 2007 by Meyer & Meyer Sport (UK) Ltd.
Aachen, Adelaide, Auckland, Budapest, Graz, Johannesburg,
New York, Olten (CH), Oxford, Singapore, Toronto
Member of the World
Sports Publishers' Association (WSPA)
www.w-s-p-a.org
Printed and bound by: B.O.S.S Druck und Medien GmbH, Germany
ISBN: 978-1-84126-213-0
E-Mail: verlag@m-m-sports.com
www.m-m-sports.com

CONTENTS

1 WHY EXERCISE WITH A HEART RATE MONITOR?

These days, the electronic measurement of the heart rate in therapeutic, fitness and competitive sport is taken for granted, and is the most important way of controlling and monitoring load intensity. However, measurement is still not really a training aid in itself. A heart rate monitor is only really useful if the user can correctly evaluate the data it measures.

In addition, many people lack the background knowledge that would allow them to make their own decisions. Knowledge of how the heart works, heart rate variations due to training, stress and health problems, will enable you to make the right decisions. Nobody can do this for you. By improving your own knowledge, you will also be able to take more responsibility for your own training. You will be able to adapt training plans to your own individual requirements, according to your performance level, current trainability and state of health. Regular measurement of your heart rate and the correct interpretation of the data will enable you to come very close to doing the right training in the right way at the right time, at the right intensity and for the right duration.

The right training load is a basic requirement used by all athletes to allow them to meet their personal goals. Perhaps you want to improve your endurance ability, lose weight or just improve your well-being. To meet these goals, it is very important to listen to your body's signals as you train and to use them for your benefit.

These goals often seem unattainable because training loads are not adapted to individual ability. If the training intensity is too low, the desired result of improving endurance will not be achieved. On the other hand, training that is too intensive with insufficient recovery, will inevitably lead to **overtraining**, and stagnating or a drop in performance. For training to be effective, it is necessary to find the optimal load intensity.

If you only assess loading using your subjective perception or estimated data, you can often make mistakes, but your heart does not "lie." It shows whether training is effective or not at the moment of testing.

The heart is an extremely sensitive organ and bears only a passing resemblance to an engine that changes revs with more power. The rhythm of the heartbeat is individual and everyone has their own rhythm. When accurately analyzed, it is like a personal fingerprint.

Resting heart rates can vary by 50-60 beats for people of the same height, weight and age. There are also big differences between the sexes, as women's heart rates are faster than men's, due to the smaller size of the female heart.

Electronic heart rate monitors measure the electrical impulse of the heart, the number of beats per minute at which the heart pumps blood into the body. The electrodes in the transmitter belt sense the heart's electrical impulse and send the information to a receiver in the form of a watch (wrist unit).

Why exactly is the heart rate (HR) such an important monitoring and control parameter for endurance sports? The HR at rest, at submaximal and maximal loads and in the recovery phase gives information about the load intensity, volume and efficiency of the cardiovascular system and the muscles. The training HR increases in a straight line within certain limits with the intake of oxygen, and therefore also with performance. The angle of increase of the HR curve gives information about the endurance ability of the athlete [6].

Since the development of the portable heart rate monitor, it has had several fields of application. It can be used as a performance diagnosis tool, a load measuring tool and as a recovery management tool. First and foremost, ongoing HR measurement helps the wearer to implement and monitor the prescribed training intensity. The HR also helps to monitor one's physical condition.

The HR offers numerous advantages compared to other parameters. It can be determined simply and accurately and can also be measured while exercising with a portable HR monitor. The continuously measured HR therefore gives a very accurate picture of our physical condition and how it changes. It is, in a manner of speaking, a reflection of the load.

Without great financial outlay, the athlete can determine his HR at any time and be informed at any moment during his workout of the stress his body is under. He himself can check whether he is performing at the desired load intensity as well as whether he is training above or below the levels required by his training program. It enables you to feel better, avoid excessive speeds and loads, monitor and optimally design the training management and planning by yourself. Thus, heart rate monitors work as excellent biofeedback and monitoring tools because they display the reactions of the heart to different factors reliably and as accurately as an ECG.

By measuring your heart rate, you will learn how to work out at the optimal intensity for your physical condition and individual performance goals. You will no longer have to rely on pure guesswork to determine how hard you train, but will be able to listen specifically to the rhythm of your own body.

Paying attention to your individual heart rate also helps to strengthen your cardiovascular system gradually and to noticeably improve your ability, so that you can meet your training goal. You will quickly be able to see individual limitations or possibilities for improvement by tracking your heart rate. The results will be a noticeable improvement in fitness, condition and well-being.

For competitive athletes who are aiming for a specific training goal, the heart rate monitor serves as a tool for fine-tuning.

So, if you are looking for an easy, effective and intelligent way to monitor your own body during loading and obtaining feedback that one normally could only get in a laboratory, then it makes sense to train with a heart-rate monitor.

There are many arguments in favor of using a heart rate monitor to manage your training:

- **Improve well-being:** If you train in your personal HR zone, you will improve your well-being and avoid overtraining.

- **More effective use of training time:** Training at the right intensity is a more effective use of training time.

- **Improve performance and fitness:** If you know your individual HR zone, you can plan your training better and more efficiently, and improve your performance more quickly.

- **Spot health problems more quickly:** If you check your HR before, during and after working out, you will spot health problems more quickly and be able to treat them immediately. This reduces the risks of physical activity.

- **Keep motivation:** Motivate yourself with the amount of calories burned in training calculated for you by the heart rate monitor.

2 THE HEART AND ITS RHYTHM

2.1 The Heart – A Sensitive Organ

The Heart – Working Non-stop

What we feel as our heart beats is the action of waves of blood, triggered by the heartbeat, hitting the vessel walls. After a long, exhausting endurance run, your breathing speeds up and you feel your heart beating more strongly. The heart ensures that the brain, organs, muscles and skin receive an adequate supply of blood via the blood vessels. The heart pumps ceaselessly, as we cannot live for more than 2-3 minutes without oxygen.

From a morphological and functional point of view, the heart is a masterstroke of nature; as the center of the circulatory system, it reacts to every demand, even from the furthest extremities of our bodies.

The heart beats from the fourth week of fetal development. With every heartbeat, it sends life-giving blood around the body. Every cell in the human body must be supplied and then evacuated – a task that the circulatory system can only manage with the help of the heart. This is as true for an unborn child as it is for a marathon runner.

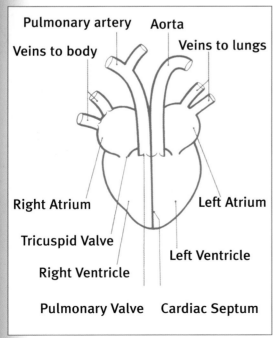

Fig. 1/2.1: Structure of the heart

An adult's heart is somewhat larger than a man's fist and weighs about 300g. It is located in the chest cavity and is almost completely surrounded by the lungs and protected by the sternum, ribs and spine, together with the ligaments and the muscles of the chest wall. An adult heart is about 6 inches long by 3 inches wide and 2.5 inches thick.

It is a hollow muscle, which contracts regularly, thereby pumping blood into the body and down special blood vessels into the heart muscles. The inside of the heart is divided into two parts by the heart wall. Each half consists of a smaller atrium and a larger ventricle, which are separated by valves. The valves allow blood to only flow one way, from the atrium to the ventricle (figure 1/2.1).

The Heart – The Tireless Pump

The heart beats about 70 times per minute at rest, which makes 100,000 beats every day and about 2,500,000 times in a human lifetime.

The actual number of beats may even be higher, as the body is active for much of the day and the heart has to beat faster to adapt the blood supply to the demands of the working muscles. The amount for people with endurance ability will be well below this though, as their hearts beat only 40-50 times per minute at rest, which represents an economy for the cardiovascular system.

An adult's blood volume makes up 8% of his bodyweight, i.e., 12 pints for a person weighing 165 lb. At rest, the heart sends out 70 ml of blood per minute (stroke volume) and about 10 pints per minute (cardiac output). That makes 17,000 pints per day. Under heavier loads, the cardiac output can even reach 80-100 pints.

The Circulation of the Blood

The atrium of the heart has thin, elastic walls and receives its blood from large veins, which then flows through the bicuspid valves into the thick-walled part of the pump, the ventricle. The heart muscle (myocardium) then squeezes the blood through two more valves into a large artery. The right pump sends the blood to give up carbon dioxide and take up oxygen in the lungs.

After flowing through the lungs, the blood arrives in the left pump, which then distributes the blood throughout the body. Once it has delivered oxygen and picked up carbon dioxide there, the blood returns to the right ventricle via the veins.

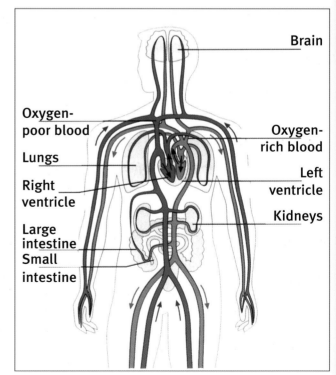

Fig. 2/2.1: The circulation of the blood

The Oxygen Requirements of the Heart

All tissue, particularly working muscles, requires oxygen. This includes the heart, a ceaselessly active muscle. It is true that a great deal of blood flows through the atria and ventricles, but it moves too fast and the muscle walls are too thick for the heart to be supplied directly by the blood that flows through it. This is why the heart also has a supply circulation: 5 % of the blood sent out by the heart is diverted for its own use.

The Electrical Stimulation of the Heart

For the heart to beat, it must be stimulated. The stimulation of the heart muscle occurs inside it, with no external influence. Even a heart that has been removed from the body will continue to beat under certain conditions.

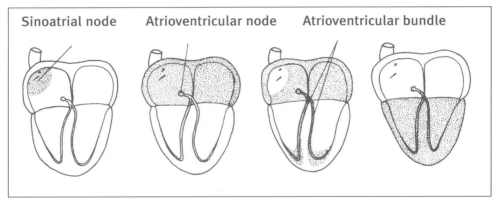

Fig. 3/2.1: Stimulation generation/sequence in the heart

The heart possesses its own system for generating electrical stimuli, which are then transferred around the whole heart. The basic rhythm of the heartbeat begins with a group of "pacemaker cells" in the right atrium, which form the sinoatrial node. The stimulus generated in the sinoatrial node not only stimulates the heart muscle, but is also transmitted to the surrounding tissue, as all body tissues are good conductors.

Although we are not aware of the stimulation passing through the heart, it does reach as far as our skin and can be measured on its surface with the appropriate equipment. It can be recorded by means of an electrocardiogram (ECG), an invaluable medical diagnostic tool. The ECG gives information about the condition, frequency and rhythm of the heart, the location, diffusion and regression of the stimulation, as well as any disruptions.

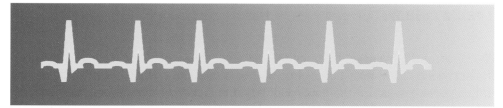

Fig. 4/2.1: Electrocardiogram (ECG) at rest

The difference between an ECG and a heart rate monitor is as follows: an ECG gives a picture of the complete heart rhythm, while the heart rate monitor only gives the duration and number of heartbeats.

The Cardiac Cycle

The heartbeat, the contraction of the myocardium and its subsequent relaxation, is called the **cardiac cycle**. A normal cardiac cycle lasts about 0.8 seconds. The contractile phase, during which blood is pumped into the large arteries, constitutes **systole**, while its relaxation phase, during which the ventricles are filled with blood, is called diastole. The activity of the heart can accordingly be divided into two groups: at the start of systole, the ventricles are stretched and filled with blood, while the atria are contracted. Heart valves prevent blood from flowing back into the afferent blood vessels. The blood is pushed through the valves into the ventricles. The process of filling the ventricles with blood is called **diastole**. Now both ventricles push together into the atria. The blood is pumped into the body and the lungs. This process is called **systole**. The pressure wave of systole is felt as the pulse in the arteries, e.g. on the wrist or at the temples. At the end of systole, the ventricles are almost empty. Meanwhile, blood from the body is streaming back into the heart. When the atria are full again, the whole process is repeated.

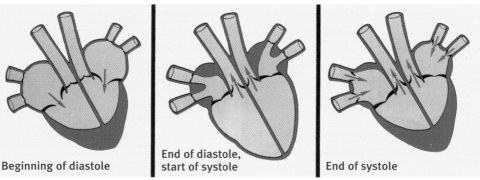

Beginning of diastole   End of diastole, start of systole   End of systole

Fig. 5/.2.1: The cardiac cycle

Stroke Volume

The heart must cover the increased oxygen requirement of an active musculoskeletal system by increasing the volume of circulating blood (the **cardiac output**). The minute output is the product of the amount of blood pumped per minute and the beats per minute (minute output = cardiac output x heart rate). The ability to increase the stroke volume is an indicator of a healthy, well-trained heart. But the heart muscle also limits, as its strength cannot be increased indefinitely. These limits are determined less by the muscle than by the coronary blood supply, which does not keep up with the growth of the muscle.

Heart Rate

The heart beats significantly faster during physical activity or mental excitement than at rest. The heart rate, i.e. the number of beats per minute, can be modified by numerous exogenous and endogenous factors (see chapter 2.7). Figure 6/2.1 illustrates this, showing factors relevant to sport.

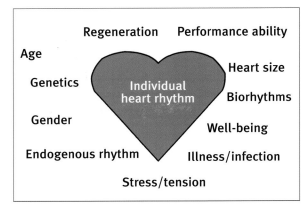

Fig. 6/2.1: Factors influencing heart rate

What Happens when Your Heart Takes it Easy?

A muscle is only efficient when it is used regularly, and this includes the heart. The best training for our cardiovascular system is regular exercise, such as endurance running, cycling or swimming. Endurance activity raises the oxygen requirement of the muscles, which is covered by an increase in heart rate and cardiac output, plus more rapid breathing.

A healthy heart will normally not suffer any damage from physical activity. Sports training must always be appropriate to the individual's performance level and trainability, and this is all the more true for those with a reduced cardiovascular function (see chapter 6.5).

2.2 Exercise to the Rhythm of Your Heartbeat

Already in the pre-natal stage of our ontogenetic development as an embryo in our mother's womb, we start, albeit unconsciously, to become familiar with movement and rhythm. Our mother's heartbeat, the sounds of her breathing and digestion, the occasionally rhythmic rocking, e.g., when walking or going upstairs, are only a few examples of the natural and unconscious experiences of movement and rhythm. From that time on, our lives are dominated by rhythm.

The fetus already moves rhythmically. Endogenous rhythms can be seen from the 21st day of pregnancy, in cardiac activity, muscle activity, the peristalsis of the intestine, the pulse, the activity of the brain, etc. All organs, muscle fibers, ganglion cells, etc., work rhythmically.

The fetus' adaptation to the rhythm of the mother and to its own rhythms means that it lives and feels these rhythms. The fetus is already able to perceive its own and its mother's rhythms. So as soon as it is born, the fetus is able to vary its movement rhythm and to differentiate it more sharply in the years that follow.

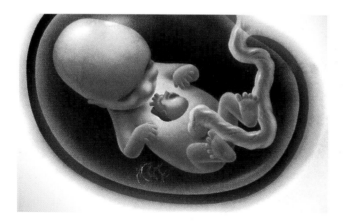

Fig. 1/2.2: The fetus perceives the mother's movement rhythm [8]

Rhythm is a basic structural element of music and is just as important as melody and harmony. In rhythm, all the forces of dynamics, gravity and tempo interact. Music therapy has proven that stress and pain, etc., can be relieved with external rhythms, such as music. In hypnosis, for example, the body's own basic rhythms of breathing and heartbeat can be used to reach a state of deep relaxation.

The Harmony of Biological Rhythms

Rhythm is the most important basic phenomenon in all biological systems. Music producers know that songs whose rhythms match the heartbeat or walking rhythm have a good chance of being successful. Our lives are marked by rhythmic cycles. Chronobiologists know of about 50 body rhythms that have their own frequencies (figure 2/2.2). The heartbeat is therefore just one of many.

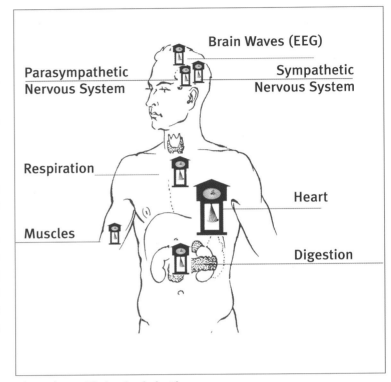

Fig. 2/2.2: Biological rhythms

It is now even possible to observe, describe, visualize and predict the complex interaction of different oscillating systems with the aid of computerized programs. Back in 1939, Erich von Holst was able to demonstrate that two principles govern physiological-rhythmic phenomena: the **magnet effect** and **interference**. When two rhythms clash, syncopation occurs, i.e., a reciprocal transient oscillation (entrainment). This allows one rhythm to be synchronized with another.

Its power of 2.4 watts makes the heart the body's strongest source of electromagnetic power. The stimulation field produced can be felt in all human cells, which is, of course, used by doctors when they measure the ECG by placing electrodes on the hands and legs. The electromagnetic field generated by the heart can also be picked up by other people, as proved by brain current measurements (EEG).

Some people can even consciously perceive the electromagnetic signals sent out by others, as reflected in such expressions as "there is tension in the air."

Within the body, the electromagnetic waves of the heart are stronger than those of the brain.

It is possible that paresthesia occurs when the different oscillations generated in the body (heart, brain, breathing) are not harmonized. Conversely, consonance (resonance, synchronicity) leads to well-being, flow-experience, creativity and many other artistic states. This type of situation can also be described as coherence. [41]

Some music therapy theories are guided by this principle, in that they try to synchronize different rhythms, be it between the heart and brain or between both sides of the brain.

The heart reacts continuously to signals from the body and the environment with finely tuned changes to the heartbeat duration and/or frequency. In this respect, the rhythm of the heart is variable and not rigid. It is constantly changing and determined by numerous endogenous and exogenous factors (see chapter 2.7).

THE HEART AND ITS RHYTHM

Running to the Rhythm of Your Heartbeat

We each have our own individual rhythm. Some athletes report that they have, some that they have not managed to find their own rhythm during competitions (running rhythm, kicking rhythm, hitting rhythm, etc.). It only rarely synchronizes with the tempo of our environment though.

Scientists have developed a technique that allows joggers to automatically adjust the tempo of music to their stride rhythm. So even though Phil Collins originally sang "Easy Lover" at a tempo of 126 beats per minute, the tempo was instantly raised to 180 bpm for sprinting. It is not the music that determines the running rhythm, but the running rhythm that determines the music. Runners can connect this system to a heart rate monitor.

If the heartbeat exceeds a pre-determined limit, the music automatically slows down, thereby also slowing the runner down. If the heart rate monitor indicates physical reserves, the music ups the pace. The runner cannot resist the rhythm coming from the headphones. This phenomenon is called the **Carpenter Effect**.

The idea of rhythmic movement automatically makes one want to move rhythmically. Many novice runners would have given up prematurely if the rhythm of the music in their headphones had not motivated them to keep running.

The activity of the heart is characterized by a regular sequence of stimuli, like the rhythm of a piece of music. The rhythmic activity of the heart begins with the opening and shutting of the valves, continues with the contraction of the heart muscle, and ends during the relaxation phase that follows the contraction.

2.3 Resting Heart Rate

The resting heart rate is measured early in the morning directly after waking up while lying in bed. The resting heart rate tells us about important changes in the body. Taking the pulse is an elementary diagnostic tool in medicine and also in sport. Even trivial health problems or ailments lead to a raised heart rate.

If the heart rate rises more than eight bpm and is combined with a lack of interest in training and abnormal fatigue, it can indicate the onset of illness. The resting heart rate can also remain high for several hours after a very intensive workout or competition. However, the following day it goes back down to the original level. If in doubt, measure your HR over a known standard distance. If you are sick, your exercise HR will be over 10 bpm higher than normal. If the elevated resting heart rate is accompanied by a fever (temperature of more than 100.4°F), you should not train at all.

The resting heart rate also tells us something about the level of endurance ability. Very well-trained endurance athletes attain values of less than 40 bpm The average value for untrained adults is around 70 bpm.

The resting heart rate for children and young people is generally an average 10 bpm higher than that of adults. Women's resting heart rate is higher than men's on average. This is mainly due to the difference in heart size, women's hearts being constitutionally smaller than men's. In order to supply enough blood to cope with the load, the woman's smaller heart must beat faster.

Exercise reduces the heart rate both in children and adults. The evaluation of the resting heart rate is important in the calculation of life expectancy, as it has been statistically proven that people with a low resting heart rate live longer than those with a constantly high heart rate, i.e., over 80 bpm.

Heart size (ml)	Heart rate (bpm)			
	Recreational athletes		Competitive athletes	
	Men	Women	Men	Women
600-700	68	72	–	–
700-800	65	68	–	50
800-900	62	65	50	45
900-1000	55	60	45	40
1000-1100	50	–	40	38
More than 1100	–	–	36	–

Fig. 1/2.3: Average resting heart rate and heart size for men and women with different fitness levels [42]

2.4 Maximal Heart Rate and Heart Rate Reserve

The maximal heart rate is the rate at which an athlete subjectively feels that he is at maximum effort. This means that the maximum load represents a state of voluntary mobilization of all strength reserves, employing the large muscle groups at the highest possible intensity. As such, the maximal heart rate denotes the temporary state of the cardiovascular and nervous systems. The maximal attainable heart rate diminishes with age. Children and young people can easily reach 200 bpm during exercise. The reduction in maximal heart rate does not affect everyone in the same way. Physically active people can still reach high heart rates into their old age. Boosting your circulation around well-trained muscles will enable you to attain higher values than those who have been inactive for several years. The age-based formula: max HR = 220 – age (in years) is usually used to calculate the maximal heart rate.

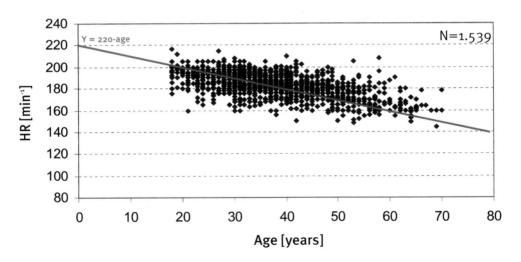

893 runners and 646 triathletes aged 18-72

Fig. 1/2.4: Maximal heart rate for runners and triathletes (own data)

However, all formulae represent a rough guide to an individual's maximal heart rate. My own research into 1,539 runners and triathletes aged from 18-72, who established their maximal heart rates with a special running test, show only a weak correlation between their age and max HR (r = -0.53). The deviation from the equation "220 – age" is ± 20 bpm for the age range 20-60 years (figure 1/2.4). In the tests, many 20-year-olds, but also a few 60-year-olds, reached a maximal heart rate of 200 bpm.

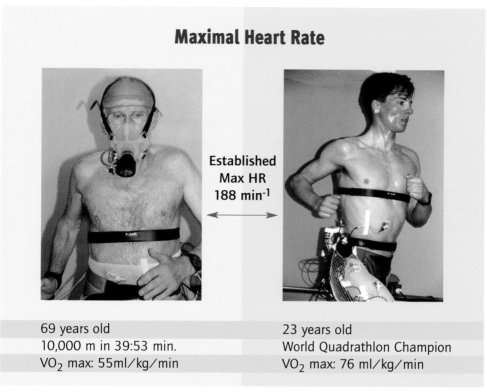

Maximal Heart Rate

Established
Max HR
188 min⁻¹

69 years old
10,000 m in 39:53 min.
VO₂ max: 55ml/kg/min

23 years old
World Quadrathlon Champion
VO₂ max: 76 ml/kg/min

Fig. 2/2.4: Maximal heart rate in endurance test for a 69 year-old and 23-year-old athlete

Establishing the Maximal Heart Rate in the Endurance Test

The intensity for endurance training should always be set after considering the actual tested individual maximal heart rate and not on the basis of a simple formula.

The most accurate way of establishing the maximal heart rate is by doing a performance test or to have it tested by a sports doctor. The pre-requisite for self-testing is that you are healthy and that, from a medical point of view, there are no contra-indications to maximal cardiovascular loading. You should not plan the test in the first two days after sickness or a long break from training. Most senior athletes should not take the test alone.

Choose a day to take the test when you are motivated and raring to go. If you participate in endurance competitions, you also reach your maximal heart rate during long sprints to the finish line.

Test Routine

1. Warm-up: 10-20 minutes

2. During the next 5 minutes, increase the exercise intensity in your preferred sport until maximal effort

3. Increase the intensity again in the final minute ("final spurt")

4. Immediately after the maximal cardiac load, read your heart rate value on the heart rate monitor display – this is your temporary HRmax

5. Then do a relaxing cool-down

Example for runners: Jog loosely for about 10-20 minutes, then start to incorporate a few acceleration runs and starts. The test distance can be 1,000 yards in a stadium, or other flat or gently sloping surface. Finish the test with a long spurt. The highest value that you can read on your heart rate monitor display is your current running HRmax.

Calculating your HRmax with a Heart Rate Monitor

If you do not wish to carry out a maximal cardiac load test, you can calculate your HRmax based on your HRrest, your resting heart rate variability, your age, gender, bodyweight and VO$_2$max. This gives a much more accurate prediction of your HRmax than if you use the age-based formula (220 – age). The calculated value is most accurate when you enter your VO$_2$max measured in a performance test into your wrist unit.

The HRmax is not only dependent on age, gender and genetic make-up, but also on motivation, muscular recruitment ability, physical fitness and the sport practiced. HRmax is a very individual value, which not only varies from person to person, but also varies during the training year and from sport to sport. If your main sport is running and you are unused to cycling, then your HRmax in a cycling test will be 10-15 bpm lower than in a HRmax running test. You should therefore always carry out the test in your main sport. This is the only way to be sure that the heart rates you end up with can be used to calculate the exercise zones for your chosen sport. The test should be repeated at regular 4-6 week intervals.

Heart Rate Reserve

The heart rate reserve is the difference between the HRrest and HRmax. Trained athletes can achieve four or five times their HRrest under loading, while untrained individuals only manage two or three times their HRrest. Someone with a low HRrest and a high HRmax will have the highest functional reserve. Well-trained young endurance athletes usually have a functional reserve of over 150 bpm. The heart rate reserve decreases as the HRrest increases and HRmax drops. For older seniors, the heart rate reserve can sink to 50 bpm or less. Performance is limited in the case of low heart rate reserves (figure 3/2.4).

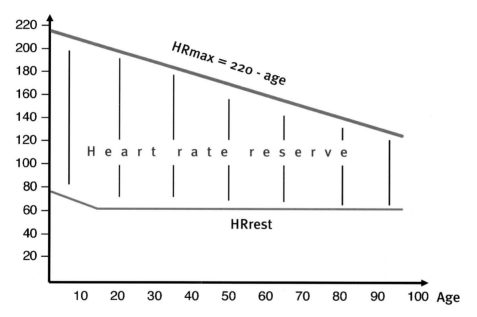

Fig. 3/2.4: Heart rate reserve at different ages

2.5 Recovery Heart Rate

The post-effort drop in heart rate is known as the recovery heart rate. For someone with a good performance level, the cardiovascular system recovers quickly after effort. The recovery heart rate is an accurate indicator of regeneration ability. If you have trained very hard or even overexerted yourself, there will be a delay in the heart rate drop. If your heart rate is still high several hours after the end of your workout, this indicates serious exhaustion and dehydration. Drink a large glass of water or isotonic drink directly after your workout. Always allow time for sufficient post-workout recovery.

The recovery HR tells us something about both the preceding load and the individual's endurance ability. The speed with which the HR drops is determined not only by the athlete's performance level, but also by the intensity and duration of the preceding workout. After an endurance competition, it can therefore take several hours for the HR to return to its starting level. The recovery HR is particularly significant if it is repeatedly measured after comparable training loads.

The drop in HR is not only dependent on the duration and intensity of the preceding muscular activity, but also on a series of other factors, such as physical condition, state of mind, body temperature, external temperature, humidity, etc. These factors must be taken into account in the evaluation of recovery behavior. The post-effort heart rate is a good indicator in the diagnosis and monitoring of health problems.

The best way to use the recovery HR to manage interval training is by using a heart rate monitor. Many monitors allow recovery to be calculated on the basis of recovery time (e.g., 60 seconds), recovery HR (e.g., 120 bpm) or recovery distance (e.g., 400m). Once the programmed recovery phase has been completed, the machine emits two beeps. The athlete then starts the next interval. When fatigue builds up during the interval training workout, the recovery distance increases, provided that the recovery calculation is based on heart rate.

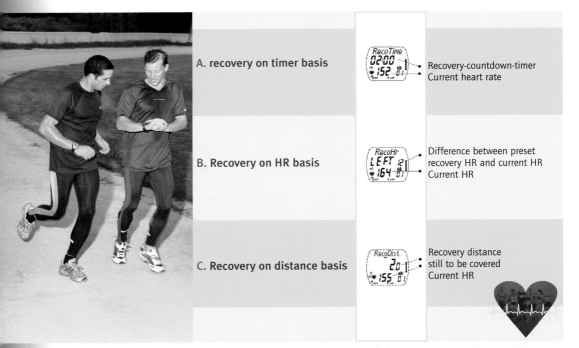

Fig. 1/2.5: Recovery calculation on timer basis (A), HR basis (B) and distance basis (C)

2.6 Heart Rate Variability

Heart rate variability (HRV) is a measurement of the neurovegetative activity and autonomous function of the heart and can be determined by the temporal change of the heart rate on the ECG or on the heart rate monitor (S 810i) with beat to beat measurement (R-R interval). While the heart rate is more informative about the quantity (intensity) of the cardiovascular demand, the HRV also provides information about the quality of the cardiovascular regulation and its influences.

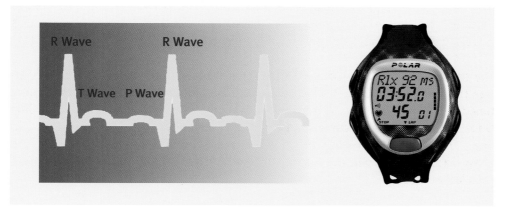

Fig. 1/.2.6: ECG and heart rate monitor S 810i. The beat-to-beat heart rate is determined by the heart period duration (R-R interval).

The heart reacts continuously to signals from the body and the environment with finely tuned variations of the heart period duration. This adaptability of the heart is based on an optimal interaction of the sympathetic and parasympathetic nervous systems. The high-frequency electrical impulses of the parasympathetic nervous system have a slowing effect and lead to a very rapid lowering of the heart rate. The low frequency impulses of the sympathetic nervous system increase the heart rate; however, the resulting rate of change in heart rate is lower than with the high frequency parasympathetic nervous system. The effect of the sympathetic stimulation requires about 20-30 heartbeats to develop fully, while those of the vagus stimulation work significantly faster. This explains, for example, the delayed HR increase at the start of physical activity, and the relatively rapid drop in HR directly after high intensity effort.

The heart rate variability of a healthy person is strongest at rest. At the start of physical activity (walking), the HRV lowers and under intensive effort (fast running), the heart not only beats faster but also very regularly, i.e., the gap between heartbeats does not vary. The heart can be said to beat steadily, i.e., there is almost no variability in the heartbeat rhythm (fig. 2/2.6).

Heart Rate Variability

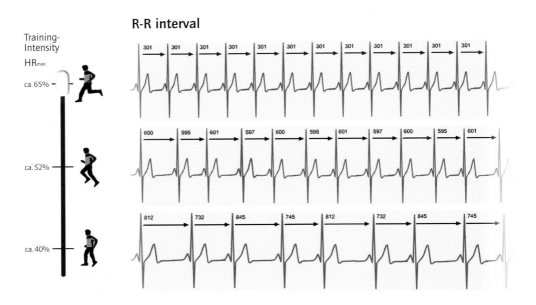

Fig. 2/2.6: Electrocardiogram (ECG) for walking, jogging and running. The heart period duration decreases with increasing effort intensity and the heart beats more evenly.

"When the heartbeat becomes as regular as the knocking of the woodpecker or the dripping of the rain on the roof, the patient will die within four days."

WANG SHUHE (3rd Century A.D.)

In healthy people, even at a resting HR of 60 bpm, the beats do not fall exactly every second or 1,000 millisecond. Variations of more than 100 milliseconds in heartbeat sequence show a normal adaptation reaction of the heart to external (exogenous) and internal (endogenous) factors. The variability of the heartbeat sequence shows the adaptability of the human body to exogenous and endogenous influences. The heart is continuously reacting to the body's inner signals and to the external demands of the environment with finely tuned variations to successive heart periods. Everyone has an individual characteristic of heart rate variability that is determined by age, gender and genetic constitution. Children's variability is greater than that of adults. Variability decreases with age.

Heart rate variability is continually changing. In a relaxed and rested state (e.g., after a holiday), the heartbeat is more variable than in a stressed state (e.g., before an exam). Research also shows that physical activity affects the HRV. Improved fitness increases the variability of the heart rate sequence (fig. 3/2.6).

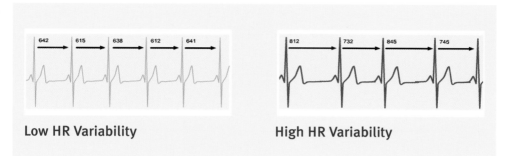

Low HR Variability   **High HR Variability**

Fig. 3/2.6: Electrocardiogram at rest of a healthy person in two different states of fitness

If we analyze the successive heart periods on the ECG or the R-R measurement with the heart rate monitor S 810i (Polar Electro) with the appropriate mathematical procedure [29], the connections between the body's regulation processes can be established, thereby telling us about the current state of stress and/or health. Sympathetic activity is predominate in cases of chronic stress. This is expressed by a low HRV. The sympathovagal balance is disturbed. A pronounced HRV is an indication of sympathovagal balance and/or good well-being and state of health (fig. 4/2.6).

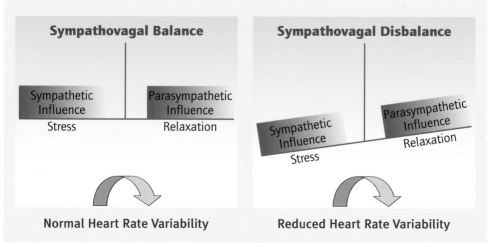

Fig. 4/2.6: Normal heart rate variability (HRV) in the case of sympathovagal balance and low HRV in the case of sympathovagal disbalance

When the body is at rest, the HRV is always greater than during exercise. This is shown clearly in the heart rate tachogram of a nine-year old child (fig 5/2.6. The heart rate oscillates steadily between 50-80 bpm. The tachogram of a 44-year-old in a state of tension looks very different. The measurements were taken immediately before a tandem jump (fig. 6/2.6).

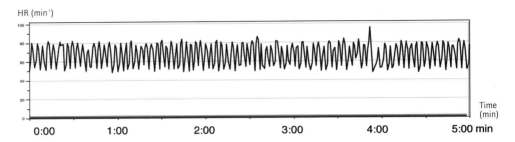

Fig. 5/2.6: Heart rate tachogram of a nine-year-old child at rest

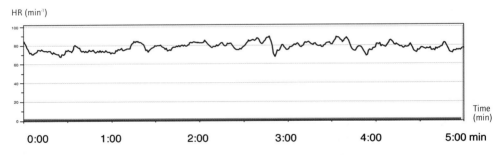

Fig. 6/2.6: Heart rate tachogram at rest of an adult in a tense, stressed state

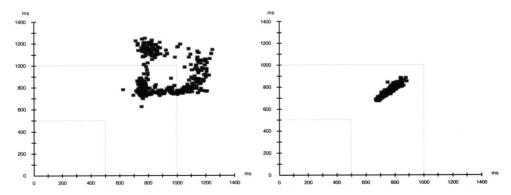

Fig. 7/2.6: Scatter diagrams of a child in a relaxed state (left) and an adult in a stressed state (right)

The scatter diagrams clearly show the differences in the HRV. We can see a high beat-to-beat variability at rest in a relaxed state (large group of dots) and a lower variability in a strongly stressed or ill state at rest (small group of dots) (fig. 7/2.6).

Factors that can lead to a reduction in HRV:

- Health problems, sickness

- Chronic stress

- Repeated high intensity training

- A series of competitions

Factors that can lead to an increase in HRV:

- Equilibrium, happiness

- Feeling good

- Moderate training

- Regeneration activities

Several scientific studies have shown that vagal activity and HRV can be increased by moderate aerobic training [21; 28]. The change in HRV can be utilized in targeted training planning. If the HRV is getting lower and lower, intensive workouts should be replaced by regenerative activities. Athletes who regularly check their HR and HRV can better tailor their training to suit themselves and more easily avoid overtraining (see chapters 3.5 and 4.8).

2.7 Special Influences on the Heart Rate and Heart Rate Variability

The HR and HRV are influenced by numerous endogenous, exogenous and constitutional factors (fig. 1/2.7). Not all parameters can be influenced. The strongest temporary changes are related to physical activity. The HR rises linearly as intensity increases and the HRV drops exponentially (chapter 3.5). The mental state also has a big effect on the HR and HRV. The emotions influence cardiac activity via the limbic system of the brain, and can raise the HR during happy experiences or stage fright for instance.

We exert a conscious influence upon the exogenous factors. The knowledge of these factors is especially important when it comes to standardizing measuring conditions. The body position (lying, sitting, standing) and the interval between meals must be the same when measurements are repeated.

The physical activity concerned must also have a similar structure. Eating raises the HR, increasing it by 8-20 bpm after lunch, for example. The HR increase depends on the type and amount of food consumed. Long periods of starvation, particularly hunger swelling, are characterized by bradycardia and low blood pressure, which are the most obvious signs of the body's altered metabolic state.

Our influence on genetic factors is limited. A reduction in the body fat percentage and improved fitness can lead to a lower resting HR and higher HRV.

HR and HRV are mainly modified by endogenous factors, such as breathing rate, breathing depth, blood pressure, body temperature and hormones. Temperature influences are mainly due to the direct effect of the temperature on the impulse-generating centers. In cases of fever, for every 1 °C rise, the HR increases by 8-10 bpm.

Factors Influencing HR and HRV

Endogenous	Constitutional	Exogenous
Breathing rate	Age	Body position
Breathing depth	Gender	Diet
Blood pressure	Body fat percentage	Stimulants
Body temperature	Weight	Physical stress
Hormones	Fitness/performance level	Mental activity
Cardiac disease	Talent	Physical activity
Other	Other	Other

Fig. 1/2.7: Factors affecting heart rate and heart rate variability

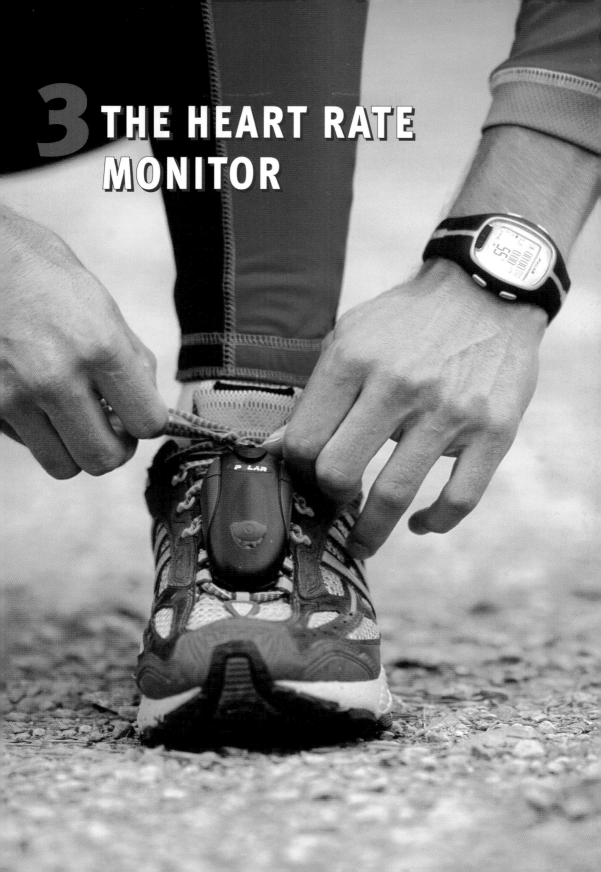

3 THE HEART RATE MONITOR

3.1 The History of the Heart Rate Monitor

Already around 300 BC, the Greeks were working on theory of the pulse and its importance for prognosis and diagnosis. In those days, the pulse rate was still measured with a water clock (clepsydra). In the past century, various inventions were made to improve pulse and heart rate measurement. The stethoscope was used for indirect cardiac auscultation, the sphygmograph, the string galvanometer, a photoelectric pulse counter or just a stopwatch to time 15, 30 or 60 seconds while the pulse was counted.

The idea behind modern heart rate monitors appeared in the 1970s. Before then, the measurement of the pulse during exercise was done by ear or fingertip contact. However, this method was neither reliable nor user-friendly, as it did not work without wires. ECG monitors, which measured the electrical activity of the heart accurately, were too big and expensive to be used in training.

The task was therefore to convert ECG technology into a portable form. After intensive research and development, the first wireless and ECG-accurate heart rate monitor was finally put on the market by the Finnish firm Polar Electro. For the first time, the heart rate could be measured during exercise with no limitations.

Fig. 1/3.1: Development of the heart rate monitor – the design ist not the only thing that has changed

The heart's electrical signal is recorded by a transmitter belt worn around the chest with integrated electrodes (transmitter) and sent to the receiver, the wrist unit. The current cardiovascular activity is permanently displayed on the watch face.

To start with, heart rate monitors were almost exclusively of interest to competitive endurance athletes. Athletes quickly recognized that by measuring and monitoring their heart rate during training, they could obtain important information about the training load that would enable them to specifically manage their training.

In the years that followed, the development and improvement of the monitors continued, so that every year, heart rate monitors advanced in technical sophistication and performance (see chapter 3.2).

The ECG-accurate determination of the duration of each heartbeat using a small, wireless heart rate monitor was an important technological innovation. The Vantage NV (Polar Electro) monitor developed in 1996 laid the foundation for determining heart rate variability (see chapter 2.6) in sports.

Today, the electronic measurement of HR and HRV in both recreational and competitive sports is taken for granted and is indispensable in the monitoring of training load intensity.

Despite this rapid technical development, there is no end in sight for the technical innovation and development of the heart rate monitor.

3.2 Functions of the Modern Heart Rate Monitor

In the beginning, only the heart rate was shown on the display of the wrist unit, but the heart rate monitor was gradually equipped with more and more different functions, determined by individual training requirements. These include the display of workout duration, average and maximal heart rate, manually set HR limits with integrated alarm if these limits are exceeded, the storage of training time in the target zone and the storage of one or more workouts.

Exercise sequences can be self-programmed so that they are tailored as much as possible to suit the individual. All settings relevant to the workout can be established well before it starts:

- Freely adjustable target zone limit values (as HR, percentage of maximal HR or as speed, depending on the monitor)

- Adjustable, varying timer

- Recovery heart rate or recovery time

- Freely programmable interval training sessions with recovery calculation after every interval and calculation of target heart rate for warm-up and cool-down

The monitor stores training data at 5-, 15- or 60-second intervals with split times and lap times. The maximal storage capacity has been increased enormously (up to 510 hours) and depends on the selected storage interval and the activated functions in the receiver.

Special functions for runners and cyclists have also been developed to optimize workouts. Using a small, light sensor in the shoe, runners can accurately determine their speed and mileage covered.

Fig. 1/3.2: The shoe sensor transmits running speed

Cyclists also have every function they could want. Along with the display of day and total mileage, wireless speed measurement and pedaling rate, personal performance can also be determined using an output meter. Pedaling technique can be improved by analyzing the right-left balance (see chapter 5.4). The heart rate monitor can even tell you the altitude, temperature or your predicted arrival time.

The functions for calculating body mass index (BMI), energy expenditure, and personal heart rate target zones help to support a successful weight-loss program and the long-term maintenance of the desired weight. To improve fitness, the athlete first establishes his own fitness level and then uses it as a basis for setting up a personal fitness program. Suggestions are made for weekly training programs, the number of workouts, the weekly calorie expenditure and exercise duration for different intensity levels.

The HR transmitter is coded to ensure that your monitor always displays your own HR during training.

Another technological upgrade consists of measuring, continuously displaying and storing the exact length of individual heartbeats. This also enables HRV to be used in exercise planning. Advances have also been made in the methods of analyzing personal performance improvement. Whereas initially only HR data could be transferred to DOS by computer interface, all data can now be transferred and analyzed by infrared data communication. This allows you to keep a comprehensive personal training diary on your computer.

Fig. 2/3.2:
Transfer of stored
heart rates

Since 2004, the most affordable models, which are most popular among recreational athletes, have offered the possibility of documenting training online by acoustic data transfer ("SonicLink"). If you need a very fast analysis of the data, you can also transmit training data from special HR monitors (e.g., Polar S625X) to your cell phone and send them by SMS to your coach or friends.

Table 1/3.2: Features available for heart rate monitors

- Switch function to training time or time of day

- One or more freely adjustable upper and lower heart rate limits and integrated alarm function if heart rate target zones are exceeded

- Stop function

- Several independent timers (e.g., for interval training) and storage of split times and the corresponding heart rate values

- Automatic calculation and display of average heart rate and HRmax

- Optional setting of recovery heart rate, recovery time or recovery distance*

- Input of personal data like age, bodyweight, height, gender, VO2 max, HRmax, activity level

- Determination of heart rate target zones based on age or heart rate variability (OwnZone®)*

- Optional storage of heart rate at 5-, 15- or 60-second intervals and storage of data in several exercise sessions

- Beat-to-beat (R-R) heart rate measurement*

- Display of heart rate variability (RLX value)*

- Optional display of daily and total mileage, pedaling/stride rate speed for cycling or running*

- Calculation of calorie expenditure

- Altimeter and thermometer function

- Determination of overall physical fitness (OwnIndex®)*

- Calculating the relaxation rate (OwnRelax®)*

* Features only available in Polar Electro heart rate monitors

3.3 Tips for Purchasing a Heart Rate Monitor

The purchase of a heart rate monitor depends on one's aims and individual needs. Recreational athletes have different requirements than competitive athletes or patients in rehabilitation.

The simplest monitor, offering continuous heart rate display on the wrist unit, can be purchased for less than $50. If you want more, you must also be prepared to pay more.

Prices are staggered according to the functions included (see table 1/3.2). Heart rate monitors that also allow data to be stored and transmitted to a computer or cell phone are the most expensive.

The variety of available options allows you to select a heart rate monitor that corresponds to your own wishes and requirements. The market leader Polar Electro offers the widest range of options.

There is a choice of about 20 different models. These are grouped into the following categories:

- **F Series:** Models that are simple and straightforward to use, specially for beginners and recreational athletes, up to models with individual calculation of heart rate target zones (OwnZone®), endurance ability (OwnIndex®) and energy expenditure (OwnCal®), specially for recreational sport and therapeutic exercise.

- **S Series, CS Series, RS Series:** Models with multiple features, particularly for the demands of competitive sports, in science or for particular sports (running, cycling).

- **AXN Series:** Heart rate monitors for outdoor activities (altimeter, barometer, compass).

- **WM Series:** Special models for weight management (program, daily diet log, training diary).

Questions to Help You Choose Your Heart Rate Monitor

The questions below will help you to choose the right heart rate monitor for you:

Which target group do I belong to?
- Beginner
- Recreational athlete
- Competitive athlete
- Rehab athlete

What do you want to use a heart rate monitor for?
- Jogging, walking, cycling, triathlon, swimming
- Speed measurement and programming of training programs for running
- Pedaling rate and speed measurement for cycling
- Outdoor activities
- Weight management
- Computer analysis

Which additional features are important for me?
- Several display rows
- OwnZone®
- OwnIndex®
- OwnCal®
- Interval trainer
- Altimeter
- Running speed

What else do I need?
- High measurement accuracy
- Low interference liability
- Ease of use
- Large, legible numbers
- Coded transmitter belt

A common problem of heart rate monitors is that they are prone to interference from electromagnetic fields like high-tension lines in the countryside or city (train, tram). This is because of their low transmitting power, which is kept deliberately low to prevent health risks.

If several athletes are wearing heart rate monitors, the monitors can interfere with each other. The heart rate displayed will then be incorrect, as interference occurs when the users are near each other. Coded transmitters were developed to avoid this kind of interference.

You should buy a heart rate monitor from a specialist shop where you can get expert advice.

3.4 First Encounter with a Heart Rate Monitor

When the first heart rate monitors were used by athletes at the end of the 1980s, most coaches were very critical of this new method of training management. Coaches were used to calculating training intensity on the basis of distance PRs. They were extremely suspicious of them and gave warnings about becoming dependent on and over-controlled by an electronic gadget.

At the time, knowledge of the use of the heart rate to manage exercise intensity was sketchy, hence the dangerous practice of athletes sticking rigidly to heart rate targets even when they were much too high. The heart rate monitor is not a technical gadget wrapped around your wrist that must be obeyed and the displayed data followed blindly.

The point is to listen to your heart, to get to know your body, interpret its reactions correctly and to incorporate them into your training program. Only when you are able to understand the measured heart rate at rest, during exercise, and in the recovery phase, in the context of your training and other influences (see chapter 2.7), will you be on the way to training efficiently and avoiding incorrect training or overtraining.

Entering Personal Data in the Heart Rate Monitor

Before you start training with the heart rate monitor, you must first enter your personal data. Once you have input your age, height, weight, gender and level of activity, the heart rate monitor calculates your personal training limits (see chapter 3.5).

Place the Transmitter Belt around the Chest

The wireless heart rate monitor consists of a transmitter (transmitter belt worn around the chest) and receiver (wrist unit). For the data to be sent with as little interference as possible, there must be good contact between the electrodes and the skin. It helps to moisten the electrodes with water. The transmitter belt must be positioned around the chest so that it fits well, not too tightly and not too loosely.

Men should place the best below the pectoral muscles, and women just below the breasts. The moistened electrodes must be placed directly on the skin and the manufacturer's logo should face outward. For accurate measurement, the electrodes should remain wet throughout the workout, which is automatically guaranteed by sweating.

Starting your Heart Rate Monitor before the Workout

a) First wrap the wrist unit around your wrist. The distance between the transmitter and receiver should be no more than 1 yard. The display shows the clock time. Before the start, make sure that there are no other people wearing heart rate monitors near you and no high tension lines, TV sets, cell phones or other electromagnetic fields that could interfere with the transmission of your heart rate to the receiver.

b) Press the OK button to start measuring your heart rate. The heart symbol will start to flash and after no more than 15 seconds, your heart rate will appear on the display in beats per minute.

c) Press the OK button again. The stopwatch will start to run and you can start training. Heart rate monitors that can store training data will only do so when the stopwatch is running.

Stop the Heart Rate Monitor after Training

If you have a heart rate monitor that can store data, you can stop the measuring and storage process by pressing the STOP button. The heart rate will still be measured though and shown on the display.

Once the heart rate monitor is switched off, remove the transmitter belt. Dry it with a towel and keep it in a clean, dry place. In chapter 3.8, you will learn more about the care and maintenance of the transmitter and receiver.

3.5 Determining Individual Heart Rate Target Zones

Scientific Background

The determination of personal heart rate target zones using the heart rate monitor is based on scientific knowledge of the behavior of heart rate variability under increasing exercise intensity. As already explained in chapter 2.6, the HRV of a healthy person is normally highest at rest, i.e., in a relaxed atmosphere and with a low resting heart rate.

Exercise leads to an increase in heart rate and a drop in HRV. The analysis of special parameters of the HRV during increasing exercise intensity can provide new insights that are relevant for training management. Fig. 1/3.5 illustrates this principle. HR and HRV show different curves under increasing exercise intensity. While the HR curve shows a linear increase, on examination, we can see that the high frequency vagal modulated HRV (SD1 value in the Poincaré Plot) reaches a "minimum HR" in the zone of around 60-70% of HRmax. This minimum can be given an HR value, which is also the reference point for calculating heart rate target zones (fig. 1/3.5).

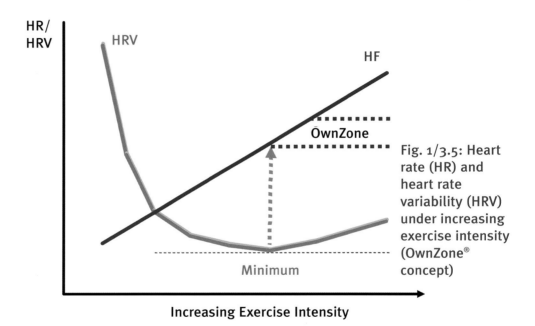

Fig. 1/3.5: Heart rate (HR) and heart rate variability (HRV) under increasing exercise intensity (OwnZone® concept)

The OwnZone® Test with Heart Rate Monitor

You can establish your OwnZone® using special heart rate monitors made by the company Polar Electro (F and RS series). The athlete does not need to carry out complicated mathematical analyses; he just needs to do a short "warm-up test" lasting a few minutes. The OwnZone® is calculated by the heart rate monitor's software. Before starting the first calculation, personal data, such as age, weight and gender, must be entered. The OwnZone® calculation should be done in a sport specific way. For example, for running, the running tempo is slowly increased every minute (fig 2/3.5). The heart rate should rise continuously, i.e., about 10-15 bpm. Novice runners should start the test by walking slowly for one minute, then walking fast for one minute and then making the transition to slow then faster jogging.

No exhausting test with maximal cardiac load is required either, just a standardized, short warm-up program before the workout, which involves starting with a very low level of activity, then increasing the intensity every minute. The OwnZone® is calculated after an average of 2.5 minutes (fig. 2/3.5).

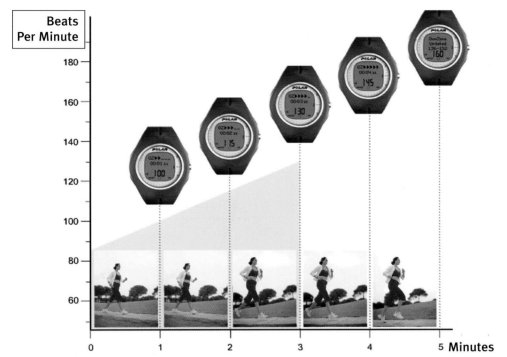

Fig. 2/3.5: The OwnZone® Test

Heart Rate Target Zones – The OwnZone® Calculation

The calculation of the OwnZone® is done automatically. The result is shown on the display of the wrist unit. There are four intensity areas that you can select from the OwnZone® function of the heart rate monitor.

OZ Basic:	ca. 65-85% of HRmax
OZ Light:	ca. 60-70% of HRmax
OZ Medium:	ca. 70-80% of HRmax
OZ Hard:	ca. 80-90% of HRmax

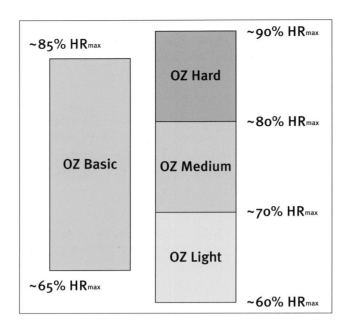

Fig. 3/3.5: OwnZone® function intensity Zones

The intensity zones change with increasing age. The heart rate zone from the lower to the upper limit within the heart rate target zone therefore reduces with decreasing heart rate reserve (see chapter 2.4). The OwnZone® is not only affected by heart rate reserve and age, but also by daily variations in performance and mood. If you are feeling relaxed and are in good shape, the OwnZone® HR values will be slightly higher than if you were in a stressed state. This difference is due to the behavior of heart rate variability, which can be reduced or increased depending on circumstances. (see chapter 2.6).

Heart rate in beats per minute

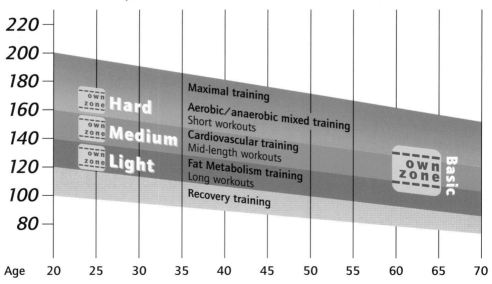

Fig. 4/3.5: Intensity zones for different endurance training goals as they relate to age

The training zones are stored in the heart monitor. The athlete chooses the zone that corresponds to their training goal. Fat metabolism training in the long duration endurance zone takes place in the OwnZone® Light and intensive endurance training in OwnZone® Hard.

In the OwnZone® Light, energy is mainly provided by activating the fat metabolism. High fat metabolic activity is attained during long workouts (> 45 minutes). In the OwnZone® Hard, the aerobic carbohydrate metabolism dominates. At the upper limits of the OwnZone® Hard, it switches, according to the athlete's training level, and anaerobic metabolism takes over.

Exercise in the individual OwnZones® is recommended for all those who want their endurance training to be healthy, stress-reducing and fitness-oriented. Beginners or the overweight should train at a lower intensity, i.e., OwnZone® Light or Basic.

You should only exercise when your body is fit and healthy. It is therefore important for every athlete to be informed as quickly and objectively as possible as to their current state of health. Training with an existing or potential infection is bad for the health and can even trigger serious complications (e.g., inflammation of the heart muscle, or myocardium). This is especially true for endurance and ball sports with high cardio-vascular loads. In cases of high family or professional stress, exercise should also provide relaxation. By doing the OwnZone® calculation before every workout, the athlete is kept informed about his current fitness level. In the case of a potential infection, the HRV drops and the HRV minimum is reached at a lower heart rate. This affects the OwnZone®. The individual training intensity is lowered, thus reducing the risk of overtraining.

Innovation in Demand-oriented Training Management

The calculation of the heart rate target zones that take into account physiological changes in the beat-to-beat interval of our heart rhythm is an innovative and very helpful way of personalizing training even more. The test is practical, easy to learn and can be repeated as often as desired (daily). Maximal effort is not required. The heart rate zones do not remain constant over weeks and months, but change from test to test according to daily form and health. This direct feedback allows the ongoing monitoring of trainability and state of health.

3.6 Determining Endurance Ability and Fitness

Endurance fitness changes with training and can be evaluated by VO_2max and the behavior of loading heart rate during training. A good state of fitness is indicated by a low heart rate during a given load. Figure 1/3.6 shows the connection between being fit and unfit.

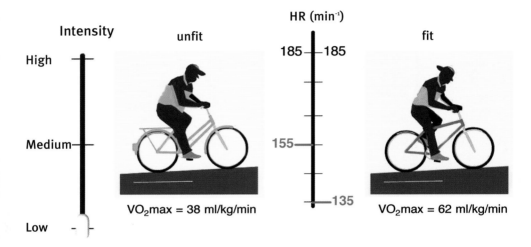

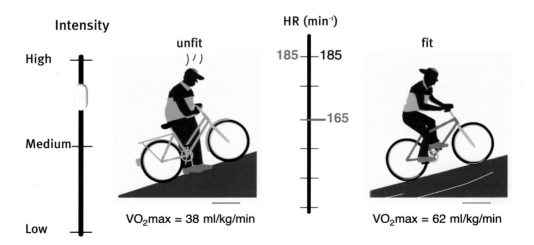

Fig. 1/3.6: Change in loading heart rate according to fitness level

The fitness and performance level of the athlete is the starting point for training planning. At the elite level, extensive diagnostic tests are carried out 2 or 3 times a year on the treadmill or bike ergometer to determine lactate levels, VO_2max, heart rate, etc. Medium-term training planning is based on the results.

Further simple tests support the short-term training planning, in order to react to immediate changes in trainability and health. These tests do not usually involve maximal cardiac loading, but the measurement of cardiovascular function during moderate exercise or at rest.

In recreational sports and therapeutic exercise, these tests are particularly important. The UKK Walking Test and the Polar OwnIndex® are proven ways of determining your endurance fitness.

The UKK Walking Test

The **UKK Walking Test** was developed by Laukkanen [32] in order to measure the aerobic fitness of healthy adults during moderate exercise. The test involves walking for 2km at a fast, but steady pace, and then measuring the time taken and heart rate at the finish.

On the basis of the time taken, heart rate at the end of the test and personal data, the "Polar Precision Performance" software calculates the person's so-called walk index and estimates the VO_2max.

This walk index can also be calculated by hand using a formula, or alternatively a Polar heart rate monitor (F5) can calculate the value automatically at the end of the test. The test result can be compared with the fitness levels of other people of the same age and gender. Performing the test regularly allows improvements in fitness to be demonstrated.

According to studies by Laukkanen, et al. [33], the 2km walking test is suitable for everyone between the ages of 20 and 65, who are not seriously ill and who have no restrictions against walking fast. The test is not suitable for children. Persons over 65 can do the test if they are healthy and work out regularly. The results are not accurate for very fit people, as it underestimates their walk index.

The Polar OwnIndex® Fitness Test

As explained in chapter 2.4, the resting heart rate informs us about our current endurance ability and fitness level. A low resting heart rate indicates good endurance ability. Determining the heart rate variability gives further meaningful indications as to the condition and regulation of the autonomous nervous system (chapter 2.6).

A particular challenge for science is to calculate cardiovascular or aerobic fitness as accurately as possible without an exhausting maximal cardiac load test. A classic linear modeling of aerobic fitness does not really work, due to the complexity and very non-linear nature of the cardiovascular system; complex mathematical modeling using artificial intelligence (neuronal networks) gives much better results [37, 36, 57, 59, 60]. Personal data, such as age, gender, height, weight, a 3-5 minute measurement of the resting heart rate and heart rate variability and self-evaluation of physical activity, are used to calculate a meaningful fitness value. The resulting value bears some relation to the VO_2max test, which is normally established by a maximal cardiac loading test.

The Polar Fitness test calculates the so-called OwnIndex®, i.e., a rest measurement lasting approximately 3-5 minutes. Before starting the test, the user's individual data and activity level must be entered into the heart rate monitor. Reliable test results can only be obtained under the following conditions:

- You must be calm and relaxed

- The test environment should be calm, i.e., with no disturbing noises (TV, phone, etc.). You should not talk during the test either.

- You should not eat a main meal, smoke or drink coffee 2-3 hours before the test

- Remember that intensive training or heavy exercise the previous day, alcoholic drinks or pharmacological stimulants affect the test results

- If the test is repeated, it should be done in the same place and at the same time of day

The Polar Fitness Test provides information about cardiovascular fitness.

Testing Process

1. Prepare the heart rate monitor for measurement (see instruction manual).

2. Lie on your back and relax for a few minutes.

3. Start the test by pushing the corresponding button on the wrist unit. Depending on your resting heart rate, the test lasts for 3-5 minutes. Remain lying down and relaxed and breathe deeply from your abdomen. Avoid any movement during the test.

4. An acoustic signal will tell you when the test has finished. The display on the wrist unit will now show your OwnIndex®.

This fitness index is very meaningful if it is used to compare your individual values and to track the changes in these values during the training process.

It should be interpreted in the context of your gender and age. Using table 1/3.6, you can evaluate your aerobic fitness compared to other people of the same age and gender.

The classification is based on an evaluation of 62 studies, which involved directly measuring the VO_2max of healthy adults in the USA, Canada and seven European countries [54].

Table 1/3.6: Classification of fitness based on relative VO_2max

	Age (Years)	1 (very low)	2 (low)	3 (moderate)	4 (average)	5 (good)	6 (very good)	7 (excellent)
Men	20-24	< 32	32-37	38-43	44-50	51-56	57-62	> 62
	25-29	< 31	31-35	36-43	43-48	49-53	54-59	> 59
	30-34	< 29	29-34	35-40	41-45	46-51	52-56	> 56
	35-39	< 28	28-32	33-38	39-43	44-48	49-54	> 54
	40-44	< 26	26-31	32-35	36-41	42-46	47-51	> 51
	45-49	< 25	25-29	30-34	35-39	40-43	44-48	> 48
	50-54	< 24	24-27	28-32	33-36	37-41	42-46	> 46
	55-59	< 22	22-26	27-30	31-34	35-39	40-43	> 43
	60-65	< 21	21-24	25-28	29-32	33-36	37-40	> 40
Women	20-24	< 27	27-31	32-36	37-41	42-46	47-51	> 51
	25-29	< 26	26-30	31-35	36-40	41-44	45-49	> 49
	30-34	< 25	25-29	30-33	34-37	38-42	43-46	> 46
	35-39	< 24	24-27	28-31	32-35	36-40	41-44	> 44
	40-44	< 22	22-25	26-29	30-33	34-37	38-41	> 41
	45-49	< 21	21-23	24-27	28-31	32-35	36-38	> 38
	50-54	< 19	19-22	23-25	26-29	30-32	33-36	> 36
	55-50	< 18	18-20	21-23	24-27	28-30	31-33	> 33
	60-65	< 16	16-18	19-21	22-24	25-27	28-30	> 30

3.7 Monitoring Relaxation and Mental Stress

Being able to relax is a basic human need. We often want to relax but are unable to. That is why many people try to learn certain relaxation and concentration techniques. Such techniques are generally based on a conscious focusing of attention away from external stimuli and onto one's own body, one's "inner" awareness. This altered perception can have definite effects on the balance of the autonomous nervous system (ANS).

A healthy heart in a relaxed state is indicated by a high heart rate variation (see chapter 2.6). The extent of the variation varies greatly from individual to individual, which is why comparisons between individuals are not really possible. Intra-individual comparisons are more meaningful (before/after). The rule tends to be: the higher the heart rate variability, the greater the physical and mental relaxation. In states of physical and mental stress, the heart rate variability decreases. Regular relaxation exercises lead to long-term adaptations like reduced sympatho-adrenal reactivity. My own studies have shown that a learned relaxation and concentration technique has a cohesive effect on the heartbeat rhythm. This is clear from the sinusoidal pattern of heart rate during the relaxation phase (fig. 1/3.7).

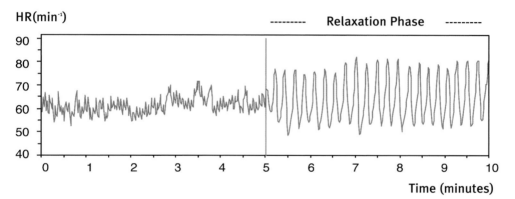

Fig. 1/3.7: Coherent heartbeat rhythm in the relaxation phase

In the relaxation phase, heart rate variability is significantly increased. The rate-analytical evaluation of the relaxation measurement shows that this is caused by an increased parasympathetic influence.

Special parameters of heart rate variability, which reflect the parasympathetic tone of the autonomous nervous system, have proven to be useful parameters for the detection of mental and physical stress when performing challenging tasks [61; 41].

A relaxation index, called the OwnRelax® value in Polar heart rate monitors, can be derived from the vagally modulated heart rate variability.

By daily self-measurement (e.g., with the OwnRelax® function of the F55 heart rate monitor by Polar Electro), everyone can find out which stressors have a particular effect on the autonomous cardiovascular regulation, and which methods (e.g., special techniques or ideas) have a beneficial, relaxing effect. The autonomous nervous system works as intermediary for opposing psychophysical organizational and emotional states, such as activation and recovery and excitement and calm.

When measuring and observing the heart rate and relaxation rate with a heart rate monitor, the person tested becomes aware of imperceptible physiological parameters of the autonomous function and is required to change the parameters in the desired way.

After a little practice, it is possible to learn how to make your heart beat more slowly or to increase heart rate variability and your relaxation rate, which reduces the oxygen requirements of the heart. These changes usually lead to a general psychophysical relaxation and also help to bring about desired specific cardiovascular effects (e.g., lowering blood pressure) in the case of underlying somatic illnesses (e.g., coronary heart disease or high blood pressure).

Relaxation Session with the Heart Rate Monitor

The measurement of relaxation with the heart rate monitor (e.g. F55 by Polar Electro) is based on the beat-to-beat measurement of the heart rate (R-R interval) at rest during a five-minute relaxation phase. The resting heart rate reflects the resting state of the body.

The lower the heart rate, the more relaxed the body is. Regular exercise also lowers the resting heart rate. Heart rate and heart rate variability are also individual parameters and vary greatly according to demand and mental stress. For this reason, the relaxation session is most useful when results are compared with previous measurements and are also interpreted while taking into account the events of the day.

Heart rate and heart rate variability are sensitive parameters in the measurement and evaluation of the general relaxation of the body. The relaxation session should be carried out at rest in a lying or sitting position. In order to be able to compare the results of successive sessions, the measurements should always take place under similar conditions.

When should the relaxation session be carried out?

- In the morning (under standard conditions), in order to determine the general state of relaxation

- Before exercising, in order to check readiness for a planned workout

- After exercising, in order to promote recovery

- Whenever you feel that you need to check your relaxation level

Start the relaxation session after adopting a calm and relaxed position. While you are carrying out the test, the word "relax" and the countdown timer appear in the display of the heart rate monitor. In the center, there is a horizontal bar that shows values from 1ms (left end of the bar) and 100ms (right end of the bar).

During the measuring process, a small vertical line appears on the bar, which indicates the current relaxation rate to the millisecond. The farther to the right this line is, the greater the temporary heart rate variability.

The yin and yang signs have symbolic value and indicate a lower relaxation on the left side of the bar (yin and yang are separate) and greater relaxation on the right side of the bar (yin and yang in harmony).

Tip: In order to train your ability to relax, you should deliberately relax so that the line moves to the right on the display (biofeedback).

Fig. 2/3.7: Result of relaxation test with the HR monitor F55 (Polar Electro)

Interpretation of the Results: Reference values based on R-R interval measurements of two large population studies in the UK and Finland involving 5,576 men and women aged 15-75, are used for the result of the relaxation session. Average values that reflect the general population are used as a reference for personal, individual results. These average values show that the OwnRelax® values are lower for older people and those with high resting heart rates. Comparisons between men and women with the same resting heart rate show that women have higher OwnRelax® values.

Using table 1/3.7, you can compare your OwnRelax® value with the resting heart rate corresponding to your age and gender. If your OwnRelax® value is lower than the average shown in the table, you are probably not relaxed enough. If your OwnRelax® value is above average, you are probably in a good state of relaxation.

Table 1/3.7: Reference values of the general population [1], [10]

	Resting HR (min-1)	45-55	55-65	65-75	75-85	85-95
MEN						
	Age (years)	OwnRelax® Values (ms)				
	25-34	39-60	32-42	23-32	15-23	11-15
	35-44	34-49	23-32	16-23	12-16	8-11
	45-54	23-34	16-24	13-18	10-14	6-8
	55-64	20-30	15-21	10-15	7-12	4-7
	65-74	18-30	13-20	10-12	5-9	4-5

WOMEN						
	Age (years)	OwnRelax® Values (ms)				
	25-34	45-69	37-52	24-34	28-24	14-18
	35-44	42-52	28-39	20-28	14-20	11-14
	45-54	30-37	21-30	15-21	10-15	7-12
	55-64	23-36	15-21	11-16	7-10	5-9
	65-74	21-35	14-20	9-13	7-9	6-7

Example: Man aged 50, resting heart rate: 60 bpm, OwnRelax® value: 34 ms.

Result: Good state of relaxation, as the value of 34 ms is above average for the general population (16-24 ms).

	Resting HR (min-1)	**45-55**	55-65	65-75	75-85	85-95
MEN						
	Age (years)	OwnRelax® Values (ms)				
	25-34	39-60	32-42	23-32	15-23	11-15
	35-44	34-49	23-32	16-23	12-16	8-11
	45-54	23-34	**16-24**	13-18	10-14	6-8
	55-64	20-30	15-21	10-15	7-12	4-7
	65-74	18-30	13-20	10-12	5-9	4-5

Tip: along with the comparison with reference values of the general population, in particular the observation of individual fluctuations and trends are important when self-monitoring.

3.8 Care and Maintenance of the Heart Rate Monitor

New generation heart rate monitors are as high tech as a computer. In order to keep the monitor in good working order for many years, you should bear a few things in mind when you use it.

The transmitter is automatically activated when you place the elasticated transmitter belt around your chest after moistening the electrodes. It switches itself off automatically when the belt is taken off. However, sweat and moisture can keep the transmitter active causing the batteries to run down faster. That is why it is important to dry off the electrodes after each use.

The belt can be cleaned with gentle soap and water. This makes the electrodes last longer. Chemicals should not be used to clean it, in order to avoid damaging the electrodes.

Between each workout, you should always store the wrist unit in a cool, dry place. Do not expose your heart rate monitor to extreme heat or cold and do not place it in direct sunlight.

If you use the heart rate monitor while swimming, the rubber seal should be replaced every 2-3 years. You should not operate any buttons under water, to avoid water getting in. The average life of a battery is about 2,500 hours.

Polar Electro offers a special maintenance service for its heart rate monitors. If service is required, depending on the model and frequency of use, after about two years, the user just sends the complete set (the transmitter belt and wrist unit) to the manufacturer. The Polar service department checks the heart rate monitor thoroughly, changes the batteries and bits and pieces and examines the display, circuit board and control of the receiver and transmitter.

4 TRAINING WITH THE HEART RATE MONITOR

4.1 The Optimal Work:Rest Ratio

In sport, the training process is characterized by systematically alternating work and rest phases plus longer recovery phases, in which the body must constantly adjust and adapt to the changing demands. The function systems involved require varying amounts of time to recover after an effective workout.

For example, the starting level of creatine phosphate is achieved after 3 minutes of regeneration, but that of muscle glycogen takes several days. It can take weeks to regenerate muscle proteins that are involved in the contraction process (tab. 1/4.1).

Tab. 1/4.1:
Regeneration time after intensive endurance loading

	Minutes	Hours	Days	Weeks
Muscular creatine phosphate reserves replenished	▮			
Normalizing of blood sugar levels	▮▮			
Lactate breakdown below 3 mmol/l	▮▮▮▮			
Fluid balance regained	▮▮▮▮▮▮▮▮			
Liver glycogen replenished	▮▮▮▮▮▮▮			
Muscle glycogen replenished	▮▮▮▮▮▮▮▮			
Muscular fat reserves (triglycerides) replenished	▮▮▮▮▮▮▮▮			
Rebuilding of dysfunctional mitochondria	▮▮▮▮▮▮▮▮▮▮			
Recovery of defenses (immune system)	▮▮▮▮▮▮▮▮▮▮▮			
Mental recovery	▮▮▮▮▮▮▮▮▮▮▮▮			

Adaptations take place at different speeds in each organ and function system. The recovery phase after high loads is faster in the fit person than in the unfit person. Well-trained endurance athletes can train nearly every day without overexerting themselves.

Tab. 2/4.1:
Weekly sequence of training (T) and rest days for different target groups

Mon	Tues	Wed	Thur	Fri	Sat	Sun	Weekly training (T) to rest ratio
Rest	T	Rest	Rest	T	Rest	T	Beginners: (1:1) and (1:2)
T	Rest	T	Rest	T	Rest	T	Recreational athletes (1:1) and (2:1)
Rest	T	T	Rest	T	T	T	Competitive athletes (2:1) and (3:1)
T	T	T	T	T	T	Rest	Elite athletes (6:1)

The cyclical loading structure ensures that the work and rest phases in the training process are coordinated. The deliberate incorporation of recovery phases into the training process allows time for the processing of training stimuli and the ongoing development of performance levels.

The work:rest (regeneration) ratio should correspond to the athlete's current trainability and performance level so that their individual adaptation potential can be realized.

Much information about the regeneration process can be obtained by measuring the heart rate at rest, during exercise and in the recovery phase. Novice runners and fun runners (joggers) require more rest days per week than competitive runners (tab. 2/4.1).

The rhythm of work and rest should not be limited to the weekly cycle, but extend throughout the whole training year and is broken down into micro-, meso- and macrocycles, i.e., 2-3 weeks of increasing the training load should be followed by a regeneration week. In principle, every training cycle ends with a recovery phase.

The duration of a cycle depends mainly on the athlete's performance level and trainability. This ensures that the training load is effective. If the training program remains unchanged for several weeks, there will be no improvement in performance.

4.2 Training Zones for Fitness and Endurance Training

Endurance ability is developed in training zones, also known as intensity zones or heart rate target zones. The aim is to raise the conditioning level. Five different zones can be used for training purposes, and each zone has a particular role and importance for the metabolism, health and development of endurance ability. The lower intensity zone trains the fat and aerobic carbohydrate metabolisms, while the upper intensity zone trains the anaerobic and alactic metabolisms. Other intensity zones focus on the transition from aerobic to anaerobic activity, for supporting recovery after exhausting workouts and for promoting physical and mental recovery.

Performance diagnostic, sports-specific tests make it possible to accurately calculate the intensity of the training zones for every athlete. The lactate level test with simultaneous heart rate measurement has established itself as the "gold standard." Very reliable intensity guidelines can also be obtained by other methods, such as the

Tab. 1/4.2:
Classification and terminology of the training zones in different sports

TZ	Intensity level	General term	Swimming	Cycling	Running	Recreational sports/ therapeutic exercise
1	Very low	Light/ Recovery	Low intensity	Active recovery	Recovery	Healthy heart
2	Low	Easy/ Fat-burning	Aerobic maintenance	Endurance	Basic endurance	Fat metabolism
3	Medium	Aerobic/ Cardiovascular	Aerobic development	Tempo	Aerobic endurance	Cardiovascular
4	High	Anaerobic threshold	Anaerobic threshold	Threshold	Anaerobic threshold	Anaerobic threshold
5	Very high	Red Line/ VO_2max	Maximal aerobic	Max effort	VO_2max	VO_2max

percentage derivation of training zones from individual maximal heart rate in the sport or OwnZone® calculation (chapter 3.5).

The names given to the training zones vary considerably for each endurance sport and for recreational sports and therapeutic exercise (tab. 1/4.2).

NB: It should not be assumed that the above training zone classifications and the attribution of training method that the intensity and loading volume are identical in each sport. The exact intensity and volume must be established for each individual sport.

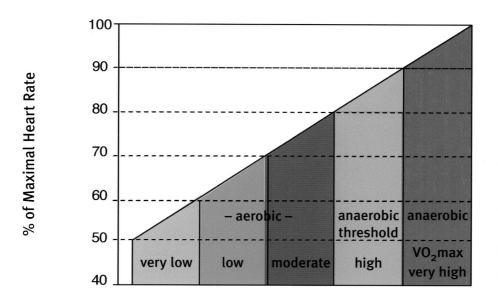

Exercise Intensity

Fig. 1/4.2: Training zones for endurance training

Training Zone 1

Recovery training (50-60% HRmax)

The loading intensity in this zone is aerobic, i.e. the oxygen in the muscle cells is sufficient to obtain energy from fats and carbohydrates. The lactate level in the blood does not rise and remains at resting lactate level (< 2.00 mmol/l). This low intensity endurance training promotes regeneration after intensive workouts or competitions and improves well-being. It is helpful in the case of health problems like high blood pressure, diabetes, cardiovascular problems and people who suffer from sleep disturbances due to high mental stress levels. The training is carried out according to the endurance method (chapter 4.4) and should last about 1 hour for cycling, 45 minutes for walking or Nordic walking and 30 minutes for running.

Training Goals:

- Improvement of general health, particularly in cases of high blood pressure, diabetes or fat metabolism disorder (metabolic syndrome)
- Promotion of regeneration and general well-being
- Overcoming mental stress
- Cardiac rehabilitation
- Warm-up and cool-down

Preferred training method: **Endurance**

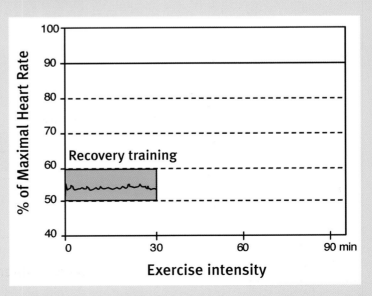

Fig. 2/4.2:
Recovery training
by the
endurance method

Training Zone 2

Fat Metabolism Training (60-70% of HRmax)

Long, low-to moderate intensity aerobic endurance loading is required for the optimal stimulation of the fat metabolism. As the exercise duration is increased (> 30 mins), the fat metabolism kicks in and the carbohydrate metabolism component decreases. This is particularly evident if, in the last hours prior to working out, no carbohydrates or energy drinks are consumed. The blood lactate level should lie in the region of about 2 mmol/l, i.e., resting lactate level.

Training in this zone promotes the development of basic endurance and improves fat metabolism activity. Training should be carried out according to the endurance method and should consist of at least 90 minutes for cycling, 60 minutes for walking or Nordic walking and 45 minutes for running.

Training Goals:

- Development of basic endurance

- Activation and improvement of fat metabolism (increase in muscle enzymes for aerobic metabolism, enlargement of mitochondria)

- Improved composition of lipids (increase in HDL cholesterol, reduction in LDL cholesterol and triglycerides)

- Economizing and stabilizing of the cardiovascular system

Preferred training method: **Endurance**

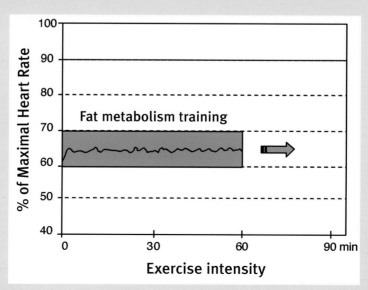

Fig. 3/4.2:
Fat metabolism
training by the
endurance method

Training Zone 3

Cardiovascular Training (70-80% of HRmax)
Endurance-trained athletes are still able to train aerobically at this intensity, i.e., their blood lactate concentration does not increase. This is not the case for untrained or overweight individuals. Their aerobic metabolism is not yet sufficiently well-developed, so that anaerobic metabolism provides some energy, even at 80% of HRmax. For this reason, in the first weeks, training should be carried out in the lower intensity zone (70-75% of HRmax) and then slowly move up to the higher intensity using the variable endurance method (chapter 4.4) or the extensive interval method (c.f. chapter 4.5). This is particularly true for cycling, walking and Nordic walking. The exercise duration should be 60-90 minutes for cycling, about 60 minutes for walking or Nordic walking and 45 minutes for running.

Changing loading intensity in particular stimulates cardiovascular efficiency and helps to improve muscle endurance and economize movement technique.

Training Goals:

- Improved basic endurance
- Improved cardiovascular efficiency
- Improved aerobic muscle endurance
- Increased aerobic capacity
- Reduced body fat percentage (weight management)
- Economical movement technique

Preferred training methods: (variable) endurance, fartlek and extensive interval

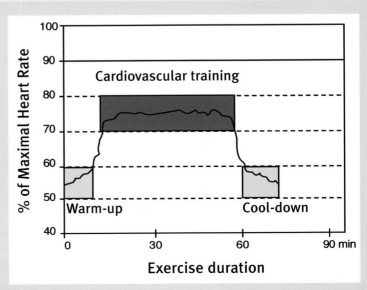

Fig. 4/4.2: Cardiovascular training by the endurance method

Training Zone 4

Anaerobic Threshold Training (80-90% of HRmax)

Endurance training in this zone can be very arduous. Only very well-trained athletes with many years training experience can manage to still run or cycle aerobically in this zone. Above 80% of HRmax, most endurance athletes have to switch to anaerobic training to cope with the speed. The anaerobic threshold can be accurately determined by a lactate level test.

This type of training forms only a small part of the weekly training cycle. Out of 4-5 workouts, only one should be in this zone. The extensive interval method (chapter 4.5) and the fartlek method (chapter 4.4) are suitable for aerobic/anaerobic threshold training. If you possess good basic endurance, training in this zone will increase your anaerobic capacity and take your endurance to a new level. The exercise duration must correspond to one's training capacity and is shorter than for zone 3.

Training Goals:

- Improved aerobic endurance
- Increased anaerobic capacity
- Formation of enzymes for glycolytic metabolism

Preferred training method: **Fartlek, extensive interval**

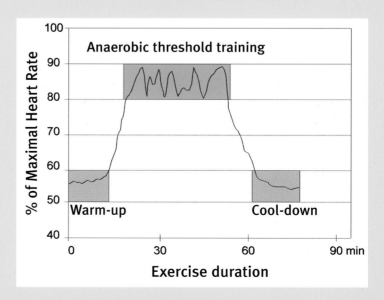

Fig. 5/4.2:
Anaerobic
threshold training
by the fartlek
method

Training Zone 5

VO$_2$ Max Training (over 90% of HRmax)

This high-intensity zone is particularly important for young competitive athletes who are aiming for good performances over short distances (competition time less than 20 minutes). It enables them to improve anaerobic performance and lactic acid breakdown. There is no point in more senior athletes or therapeutic exercisers doing endurance training at more than 90% HRmax, as there is a high risk of overloading. Very intensive training also requires the athlete to be in very good shape. Most senior athletes should not train in this zone without first having a medical check-up. This does not include sprints over 30-50 yards or acceleration runs over 80 yards as they do not make strong demands on the anaerobic metabolism. Short runs after a good warm-up recruit the whole range of muscle fibers, so that the fast fibers are available when needed and do not atrophy.

Training Goals:

- Increased competition speed
- Increased anaerobic efficiency
- Improved lactate tolerance and lactate break-down
- Recruiting fast-twitch muscle fibers

Preferred training methods: **Intensive interval, fartlek and tempo**

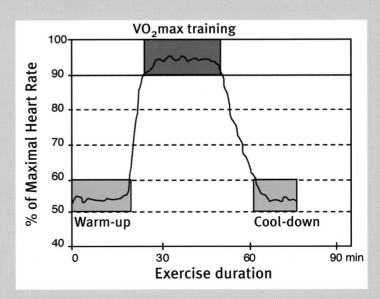

Fig. 6/4.2:
VO$_2$max training
by the
tempo method

4.3 Training by Heart Rate Formulae

Various attempts have been made over the years to use heart rate formulae to determine optimal training intensity.

• **Training HR=**	180 – age in years
• **Training HR=**	180 – age in years plus 5 heartbeats/ decade after age 30
• **Training HR=**	170 – age in years
• **Training HR=**	180 – age in years for young people and trained athletes
• **Upper Training HR=**	200 – age in years
• **Training HR=**	(HRmax-HR rest) x % training intensity + HR rest

However, these general rules do not take into account genetic predisposition, gender, performance ability, training capacity, type of sport or training goal, which are crucial factors in the calculation of individual training intensity.

Calculating training intensity solely on the basis of age and age-related maximal heart rate is not sufficient (chapter 2.4). Well-trained individuals usually attain a higher age-related heart rate than untrained individuals. Women usually have higher heart rates than men in lower intensity zones.

Endurance training takes place in different exercise zones, i.e., training heart rates depend on the training goal (recovery training, fat metabolism training, VO_2max training, etc.). The optimal training intensity can therefore only be determined after considering the training goal, not by using blanket formulae, as was previously the custom.

The uncertainty about predicting the right training heart rate is the reason why the heart rate should be measured continuously and its changes interpreted according to sports and training methodologies. In sports medicine and sports science, there are now many ways of accurately calculating heart rate zones for endurance training, so there is no longer any point in training according to blanket heart rate formulae.

4.4 Training by the Endurance Method

The **continuous endurance** method is the most popular training method in endurance and recreational sports. It is characterized by a continuous load with no rest and the maintenance of a certain training intensity over a long distance. The intensity zone is calculated by inputting the upper and lower HR limits. An acoustic signal beeps as soon as the loading HR exceeds these limits, thereby regulating the training HR speed. On hilly training routes, the pace must be varied so as not to exceed the HR zone, and a somewhat wider heart rate training zone should be programmed. On flat training surfaces or when running in the mountains, it is easy to stick to relatively narrow limits.

It should be noted that with increasing exercise duration and an unchanging heart rate, the pace will gradually slow down. This is mainly due to a rise in body temperature and increasing muscle fatigue, which require great biological effort and speed up the heart rate while the exercise intensity remains the same. The endurance method is mainly used for fat metabolism, aerobic and strength endurance training. The exercise duration should be at least 30 minutes at low to moderate intensity (65-86% of HRmax) (fig. 1 and 2/4.4).

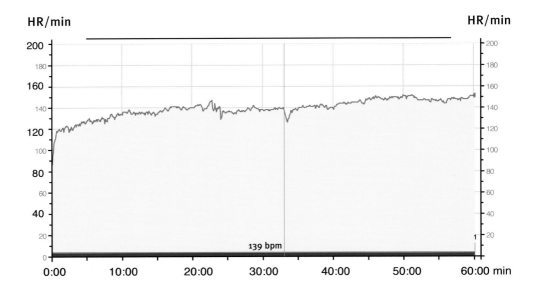

Fig. 1/4.4: Chronological heart rate gradient during running training by the endurance method. The heart rate increases due to the heat while the running pace remains the same.

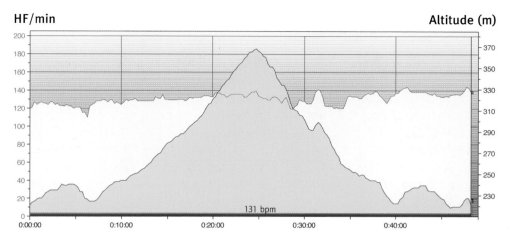

Fig. 2/4.4: Chronological heart rate and altitude gradients during KA1-mountain running training. The preset HR limits are not exceeded when running uphill.

The pace change method differs from the continuous endurance method in that different sections are run at different speeds. There are no rest breaks. As before, the training intensity can be monitored by setting heart rate limits (fig. 3/4.4).

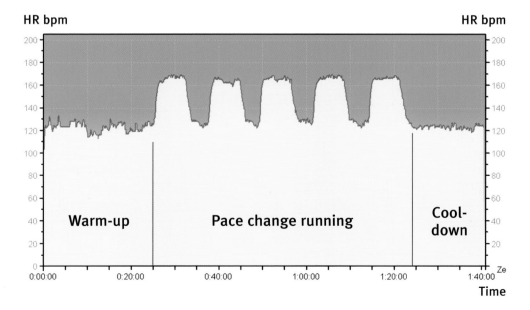

Fig. 3/4.4: Pace change method. After about 25 minutes warm-up, aerobic endurance pace (zone 2) is interspersed with several changes to cardiovascular endurance (zone 3).

The **fartlek** method is a particular form of endurance training with frequently changing pace over sections of different length. The changes in exercise intensity are not planned in advance; they are largely intuitive, based on how the runner feels. HR limits are largely irrelevant in this case, but an upper limit prevents overloading (fig. 4/4.4).

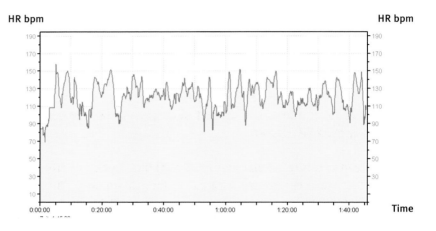

Fig. 4/4.4: Use of the fartlek method in endurance Zones 2-3 for mountain biking

4.5 Heart Rate Monitored Interval Training

The interval method is characterized by a systematic alternation of loading and recovery phases. Unlike the recovery method, the rests are not long enough to allow complete recovery, hence the significance of HR regulation between training phases. The length of the rests depends on how steep the drop in HR is. In interval training, the rest is not intended to lead to complete cardiovascular recovery, but just to be a welcome break.

Directly after the training phase, there is a quick cardiac and respiratory recovery. The heart rate drops from about 180-200 bpm to about 120-140 bpm in the first minute. The new loading starts after this partial recovery. If the HR recovery value drops from interval to interval, the recovery time is either too short or the training intensity too high.

By determining the intensity, volume and duration of individual workouts, as well as the duration and type of rest, the interval method can be specifically used to develop competition-specific partial performance and anaerobic endurance ability.

Interval training requires knowledge of training methodology. It is not uncommon for interval training to lead to physical overexertion, overtraining and a drop in performance. Usually only experienced athletes are able to train using the interval method at the right intensity for their level of performance. Many athletes overexert themselves and do not know how to structure an effective interval program.

A heart rate monitor enables the consistent control of work and rest phases. The recovery heart rate is a suitable parameter for reflecting the increasing fatigue from interval to interval. If there is a set recovery heart rate (e.g., 120 bpm), recovery time will increase once fatigue sets in. If the rest duration is to be kept constant, then the training intensity must be reduced.

Some heart rate monitors (e.g. Polar Electro S625X) have optional settings for recovery heart rate, recovery time or recovery distance for interval training. The athlete can use these settings to program his own interval training. The setting chosen depends on the training goal. Beginners can use programs pre-stored in the heart rate monitor. These options enable the implementation and subsequent analysis of performance-oriented training. Calculating the intensity and duration of each load and the length and type of recovery requires knowledge of training methodology.

Frequent use of the heart rate monitor will give the athlete a wide-range of experiences of the reaction of their body to intensive training stimuli. They will therefore not be overwhelmed when it comes to interval training; it can be used by anyone and adapted to their level and requirements. The heart monitor becomes their personal trainer.

The interval training goal can be reached more quickly and training can be more varied, of higher quality and more enjoyable. There is no upper age limit for monitored interval training. Those new to endurance sport can use the heart rate controlled extensive interval method (e.g., alternating running and walking) to avoid the often-criticized monotony of endurance training.

Heart rate controlled interval training will allow you to meet the following goals:

- feeling for different paces
- familiarity with race pace
- gaining will power, stamina and speed endurance
- form tapering and development of competition-level performance

- improved lactate breakdown and tolerance
- maintenance and improvement of technique (e.g., running style)
- increasing anaerobic capacity
- raise performance to individual limits

The volume and frequency depend on the training phase in the annual cycle, the type of sport, one's age, musculature (slow twitch, fast twitch ratio), training philosophy, etc.

Interval training can be divided into extensive and intensive methods. The extensive method, unlike the intensive method, features low exercise intensity, a high training volume and shorter rests. It is used to develop strength and aerobic endurance ability and is used with moderate training intensity in the anaerobic threshold zone (zone 4). The duration of the recovery phase depends on the duration of the intervals.

The intensive interval method develops speed endurance, using high sub-maximal running speeds, short intervals (20-90 seconds) and sufficient recovery breaks. In the intensive interval method, the loading HR is not so important in determining the intensity, as the intensity is mainly determined by speed. This can be derived from field or competition tests or by subjective impression of effort.

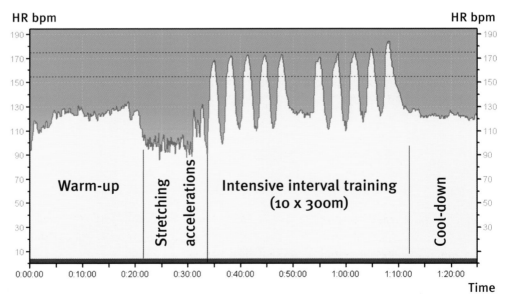

Fig.1/4.5: Intensive interval training for running 12 x 1 min and about 2 mins active recovery. The interval phase follows a 20-minute warm-up of jogging, loosening exercises and several acceleration runs. A 30-minute cool-down run finishes off the workout.

4.6 Training by the Repetition and Tempo Methods

The definition of the repetition method is that the recovery between repetitions leads to an almost complete recovery. The loading phases are short and intensive, leading to a high accumulation of lactic acid. In endurance training, it is used to develop competition-specific endurance ability and speed endurance. If the load duration per recovery amounts to several minutes, the loading heart rate serves as a reference value. In any case, the recovery heart rate should be measured during the rest to evaluate the total load. The planned training program should be adapted to the individual's trainability.

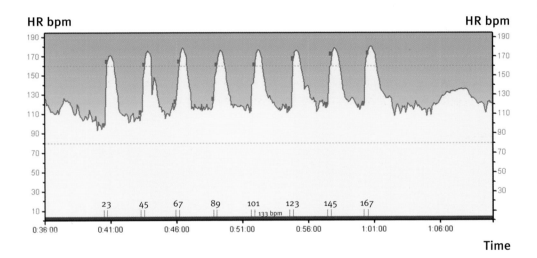

Fig. 1/.4.6: Heart rate during the repetition method

The race pace method enables the development and testing of complex and competition-specific endurance ability. Training largely corresponds to the competitive situation. It includes time trials and competition tests.

The competition tests serve to develop complex competition performance and give athletes and coaches a reliable indication of current performance levels. The use of the race pace method is geared toward peaking for the most important competition of the season. Favored methods are under- and over-distance runs, runs with training partners or runs with certain tactical requirements.

4.7 Heart Rate Measurement during Competition

Athletes of all levels use heart rate monitors during competitions. The beeping of wrist units has long been commonplace during marathons. If you set the right HR zone for the race, you don't need a split time chart. The athlete can concentrate on the reactions of his cardiovascular system and become familiar with the load.

The effects of energy and fluid uptake and cooling the head with water and sponges are directly expressed in the HR values. The current competition HR gives motivation and inspiration to maintain or increase pace, for who wants to let their HR value drop below the set zone? After the competition, the analysis of the HR curve can be interpreted in many different ways.

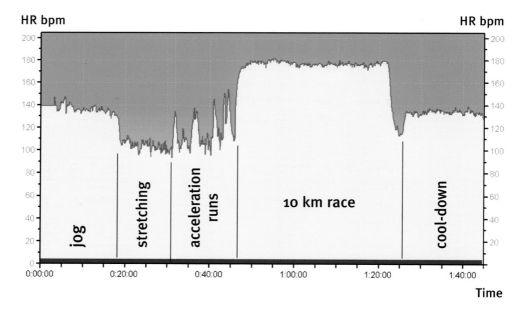

Fig. 1/.4.7: After a 45-minute warm-up (jog, loosening exercises, acceleration runs), a 10km race is run on a flat surface. A 15-minute cool-down follows the race.

4.8 The Keeps U Fit™ Own Training Program

The preparation of the training plan is extremely important. If you don't know the laws and principles of training or their effects and adaptations, you have little chance of preparing a plan that is tailored to your own goals and performance level. If you have no knowledge of systematic training planning and are unsure of how to put it into practice, you need a personal trainer.

The training plan contains volume, duration and intensity values for individual workouts, which have different effects on different people. There is comprehensive scientific knowledge available [2] about training-conditioned changes to cardiovascular fitness and VO_2max all of which influence individual training planning. Each person is a bio-psycho-social entity, which means training loads will affect them in complex, individual ways that cannot be exactly predicted [11]. For this reason, it is important to continually record exercise-induced changes. The heart rate monitor enables you to do this.

It also helps in the preparation and implementation of the training plan. The Polar Keeps U Fit™ Own Training program (e.g., in heart rate monitor F11) is a training planner based on the user's personal information. The athlete can use the monitor to track both the result of the program and the changes in his aerobic fitness.

The Keeps U Fit™ Own Training Program is a training aid that enables the user to prepare a personal training program to improve or maintain cardiovascular fitness. The program recommendation is based on the oxygen uptake capacity (VO_2max or Polar OwnIndex® fitness test).

The program initially advises the user to determine his current fitness, either manually by carrying out the Polar OwnIndex® fitness test or by direct measurement of VO_2max, in order to find out how much his fitness can or should be improved. The next step is for the user to choose the goal of his endurance program (maintenance, improvement, maximization) and the third step is to define the number of workouts that he can realistically do each week. The program is then worked out based on the above calculations and on the user's age. The program gives advice as to how the selected goal can be achieved. It recommends a certain number of workouts per week of varying duration (short, normal, long) and of varying intensity. In addition, it provides the calorie expenditure for each goal and suggests how the workouts can be sequenced.

The length of the workouts depends on the program goal (maintenance, increasing, maximizing) and the number of workouts per week (from 1 to 6+1 sessions). The short workout is shorter than the normal one, which in turn is shorter than the long one. The shortest short workout should last 25minutes and longest long workout should last 1 hour and 55 minutes.

The Maintenance Program aims to maintain the current fitness level. For those who are untrained and would like to start doing regular exercise, this program is ideal to start off with. The maintenance program consists of 2-3 workouts lasting from 30-50 minutes. This program typically involves 1.5 total training hours per week, of a low to moderate intensity.

The Improvement Program is suitable for those who would like to improve their endurance ability and who already work out regularly. The improvement program consists of 3-5 weekly workouts, with the duration of the normal workout being 40-60 minutes. This program requires an average of three hours of training per week, and includes all intensities, although most are moderate. The number of training weeks required to improve your fitness by one stage depends on the individual, and especially on the existing performance level and genetic factors. It normally takes athletes of average fitness and talent at least 8-10 weeks to improve their maximal endurance ability by 10-15%.

The Maximization Program is the right choice if you want to maximize you current fitness level. This program is suitable for people who have already been exercising for 10-12 weeks and would like to keep training regularly. The weekly duration is usually about 4.5 hours; spread over 4-6 workouts, with the duration of the normal workout being 50-70 minutes. This program uses all intensities, and the percentage of high intensity training is greater than in the other programs (10-20%).

The Keeps U Fit™ Own Training program offers a weekly training volume based on frequency (number of workouts), the total duration (hours, minutes) and the calorie expenditure. The workouts should be carried out at varying intensities: easy (< 70% HRmax), medium (70-80% HRmax) and hard (80-90% HRmax).

The higher the intensity, the shorter the duration. A short workout is usually intensive (80-90% HRmax), a normal workout is usually medium (70-80% HRmax) and a long workout is easy (< 70% HRmax). These three intensity zones can be calculated based on actual or estimated maximal heart rate or by using the current Polar OwnZone® during training, in order to get individual, daily recommendations.

The workouts are classified in the program so that the same workouts (hard/light/medium) do not follow each other directly and there are a few days between two hard workouts. This function makes the program easier to complete, guarantees sufficient recovery time and avoids overtraining.

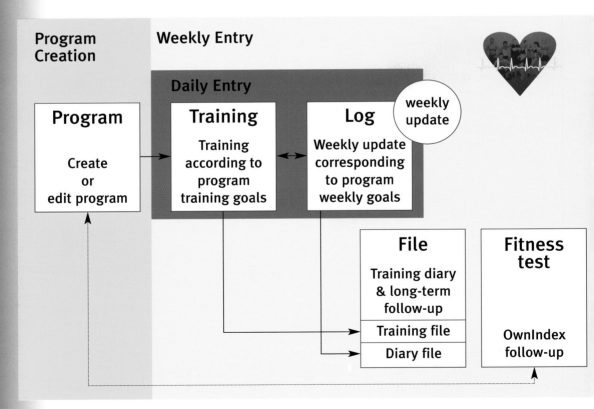

Fig. 1/4.8:
Polar Keeps U Fit™ own Training Program – overview [34]

During Training

It is recommended that you determine your OwnZone® at the start of the workout so that you train at the right intensity. This is important if you change training venue or sport, if you feel tired or stressed and if two people are sharing the monitor and personal data is changed. Alternatively, you can use the limits that are manually entered or automatically calculated by the age formula (220-age in years).

During the workout, as well as seeing the heart rate or accumulated calorie expenditure, the user can track the training duration, heart rate target zone, the time spent in the target zone, the time of day or the training goal (calories, time) of the current workout.

After Training

After the workout, the electronic diary displays the information gathered during the workout (automatic once the monitor is stopped and in the file) and the weekly summary. The diary contains the number of workouts (exercise counter), the total duration of all workouts (time), the calories expended and the duration of the different target intensities and the actual values achieved compared to the target values. The weekly feedback shows the user how close they have come to meeting the weekly goal (in terms of percentage).

Target Groups

The Keeps U Fit™ Own training program, with its update method (OwnIndex®) and alternative exercise durations (short, medium, long), are suited to endurance sports like walking, Nordic walking, jogging, running, cycling, swimming, cross-country skiing, rowing or aerobics classes.

If the wider intensity zone (OwnZone® Basic) is used, the user can also include other endurance activities in the training plan. The program is not suitable for beginners. It motivates and helps the user to meet his long-term training goals.

Understanding Training Connections

In order to understand the Keeps U Fit™ OwnTraining program and to adapt it to the individual, the user must be aware of the significance and interconnectedness of exercise frequency, duration and intensity. Regularity is the key. More often is better than less often, too often leads to exhaustion and increases the risk of injury. Training should always start with a warm-up and finish with a cool-down (chapter 5.1).

The longer you train, the more energy will be used than during workouts with the same intensity but shorter duration. That forms the basis for the structure and naming of the workouts. The higher the intensity, the more energy is used. The high intensity workouts are shorter in duration than the other workouts in order to avoid overloading.

5 DESIGNING A WORKOUT FOR DIFFERENT SPORTS

5.1 Designing a Workout: Warm-up and Cool-down

Constructing a Workout

A workout can be divided into three main parts: the warm-up phase, the main phase and the cool-down phase. Many athletes start their workout too intensively, thus mobilizing the anaerobic metabolism and repressing the fat metabolism. To prevent this happening, it is a good idea to determine the duration and the HR limit values for the warm-up and cool-down program beforehand and to program them into the wrist unit. The heart rate monitor (e.g., Polar S 625 X) calculates the average and maximal heart rate for the warm-up and cool-down phases. Fig. 1/4.5 shows how a sample interval workout is designed using the heart rate graph.

The workout or competition preparation and follow-up with a special warm-up and cool-down is essential for every athlete. Peak athletic performance cannot obviously not be achieved from a state of rest. The athlete must prepare for it in various specific ways. Even if they sometimes just seem like simple rituals, the purpose of the warm-up and cool-down are clearly visible (tab. 1/5.1).

The warm-up improves and optimizes the physical and mental state to prepare for the coming load. The optimization of the state of preparation involves central nervous (mental) activation and the activation of the body's function systems, i.e., muscles, joints, cardiovascular and breathing system. The goal of the warm-up is primarily to accelerate regeneration after high loading.

Tab. 1/5.1: Goals, methods and effects of the warm-up and cool-down [43]

Goal	Methods	Effects
Preparation for physical performance	• steady, dynamic aerobic load (e.g., 10-20 mins jog) • muscle loosening • muscle and tendon stretching • sport-specific coordination and speed drills	• adapting the cardiovascular system, metabolism (fat metabolism activation), hormonal system and motor function to the demands of higher performance level • warming up the muscles • protecting against injury • facilitation of the special motor function
Central nervous (mental) activation	• mentally focusing on the load • consciously rehearsing the movement sequence • anticipation of how the race will be run (tactics)	• increased alertness • control of the state of excitement • increased readiness to compete
Support for regeneration	• steady, dynamic aerobic load (e.g., 10-20 min jog)	• mental relaxation • muscle relaxation • faster lactate breakdown

Warm-up Methods

The warm-up always includes whole-body exercises that are mainly aerobic and last about 10-30 minutes (up to 45 minutes before highly intensive competitions or workouts). Many athletes perform tendon and muscle stretching exercises after the general warm-up phase.

The effects of the stretching in the context of the warm-up are not generally considered to be positive. Experimental findings show that long, static stretching can have a negative effect on muscular performance. For example, maximal and speed strength both decrease following intensive static stretching. The findings on the effect of stretching and the risk of injury are varied. Whereas old studies showed a clear connection between muscle stretching and the reduction of injury, newer studies show very little or no connection. In principle, intensive stretching during warm-up only makes sense for those sports or disciplines in which the forthcoming performance depends on above-average flexibility. For the endurance athlete, stretching does not need to follow the general warm-up phase, as long as the main phase does not involve intensive intervals.

The special coordination and speed drills that come directly after the general warm-up are very important. They facilitate the special motor function and prepare specifically for ensuing, intensive loads. Classic examples of this are acceleration runs.

Cool-down Methods

The cool-down phase is the transition from the loading phase to the recovery phase. All active forms of cool-down loosen the muscles and accelerate lactate breakdown. The lactate formed in the muscles is broken down more quickly by activity than inactivity.

If the external temperature is low, it is advisable to change your clothes before cooling down. The dry clothes protect against accidental hypothermia. Overcooling is only usually subjectively noticed after 15 minutes of recovery. The cool-down intensity should be low at 60-70% of HRmax.

The stretching of muscles and tendons after the general cool-down (jog) has advantages: it reduces tonicity and residual contractions. Additional useful cool-down measures include: massage, sauna, a warm shower and mental relaxation techniques.

5.2 Walking and Nordic Walking – The Ideal Lifetime Sports

Endurance is required everywhere nowadays: at school, at work, doing the chores at home or in sports. If you train your endurance, you are creating a resource that will help you to overcome the demands of everyday life while increasing your performance ability and your physical and mental resilience. Endurance means the ability to cope with continuous loads on the body and delay a drop in performance level caused by fatigue.

Which sports are particularly suited for training your endurance? They are sports that can be done anywhere and are easy to learn, do not overload the support and locomotor system and provide sufficient loading stimulus for the body, particularly the cardiovascular system and the muscles. Examples are running, cycling, inline skating, swimming, cross-country skiing, walking and Nordic walking. The latter can be termed the "gentle exercises." Their beneficial effect on the cardiovascular system and the metabolism makes them a very valuable part of any fitness program. Walking and Nordic walking provide adequate stimulation, but with no risk of overloading. Their relatively simple and natural movement patterns, the minimal cost of equipment, the high cardiovascular training effect with low pressure load on the heart and evenness of effort distribution all make walking a healthy form of exercise.

The technique of Nordic walking limits movement speed so that the risk of injury and the danger of overloading are reduced. Together with the positive effect on the well-being, Nordic walking and walking are ideal forms of therapeutic exercise for beginners, returners, seniors, the movement-impaired, the overweight and risk groups (e.g., coronary sports groups).

Characteristics of Nordic Walking

Nordic walking is a variation of walking, which resembles cross-country skiing in that the use of poles specially developed for the sport make it a very effective total body training sport. Nordic walking is the trend sport of the new century in the USA and, to a lesser extent, northern and central Europe. After the jogging and walking boom of the 80s and 90s, Nordic walking has proven to be an alternative to walking and jogging for ever greater numbers of people. The many special benefits of Nordic walking mean that it is becoming more established and less of a passing fad.

A number of studies have shown that moderate, regular walking or Nordic walking in senior and untrained people produces a noticeable rise in VO_2max, a drop in sub-maximal heart rate and resting heart rate and an increase in heart rate variability [12, 35,28].

Simple, Quick-to-learn Technique

Nordic walking technique is similar to that of normal walking and is simple to learn. Compared to walking, the arm action is more intensive due to the use of poles. The technique is comparable to the diagonal stride technique of cross-country skiing [26]. As the pole is swung back, the grip is loosened, the pole hangs loosely in the straps. In this phase, arms, shoulder and upper body muscles are in a state of optimal relaxation. As the arm swings forward, the pole is gripped again just before it is stuck in the ground. The pole points diagonally backward in the process and the ends of the pole do not swing in front of the body. In the subsequent pulling phase, the arm pulls back with the elbows slightly bent. Once they have passed the body, the pushing phase starts, characterized by a strong push of the arm back behind the hip. The elbow is locked throughout. With this push, the hand opens, the muscles relax and the arm swings loosely forward. The use of the poles also controls the stride length. The more intensively the poles are used, the longer the stride length. The leg action is the same as for normal walking. Long strides require a dynamic arm action with a wide range of movement.

Moderate Cardiovascular Demand for an Average Metabolic Rate

Untrained people can reach 60% of VO_2max and 70% of HRmax with moderate effort. This is an optimal load intensity for health-promoting exercise. Even for better trained recreational athletes, such an intensity zone is certainly possible, but requires a very quick pace. At a walking speed of 4.8 km/h on a flat surface, the relative oxygen uptake, independent of age, gender and performance level/ability, is about 13ml/min/kg bodyweight [52]. For a young man under the age of 30, this corresponds to about 25-35% of VO_2max, for older people, 50-60% of VO_2max. This means that, even when walking slowly, seniors (> 65) can exercise effectively.

With a dynamic arm action and/or through the additional use of weights, the muscular and cardiac demand and metabolic rate increases by 10-20%.

Relaxation and Well-being

Along with the purely physical load, a particular feature of the sport is the mental relaxation it offers. The steady, cyclical action with low load intensity makes it possible to reflect on one's feelings, dreams and thoughts. During this light physical activity in which the brain is optimally supplied with oxygen, it is not unusual for mental tasks to be achieved more easily and problem-solving ideas to be more forthcoming than they would be achieved under mental-cognitive stress. A long stroll in pleasant surroundings promotes well-being and has a long-lasting beneficial effect on the psyche.

Equipment and Training Design

The beginner requires functional clothing, the right poles and a heart rate monitor to check loading. The poles should be the right length, and the straps should be easy to slip around the wrist, easy to regulate, strongly attached to the pole, resistant and made of slightly elasticated material. The grip should be ergonomic, and there should be an attachable tip for roads. High-tech materials to reduce weight and vibration are of secondary importance. The pole length should be about 70% of the body height, but well-trained individuals can choose a somewhat longer pole.

However, if you only carry the poles and don't use them actively to avoid exerting yourself too much, there will be little positive effect on cardio-pulmonary performance, muscle endurance or fat loss. In walking, unlike jogging, the problem is not overloading, but underloading. Wearing the heart rate monitor helps one walk briskly, and it guarantees a minimum intensity. To start with, a load on flat terrain of 30-40 minutes 3 times per week in the OwnZone® Light and at 60-70% of HRmax is recommended.

Not all shoes are suitable for Nordic walking. The shoe must support the natural rolling motion of the foot, be flexible, and provide a good fit and optimal heel support. When walking over rough terrain, the sole must have good grip. The upper part of the shoe must be waterproof and breathable.

Normally, Nordic walking does not cause any orthopedic problems. However, if you are untrained and suddenly start walking several times a week or have not sufficiently mastered the technique, you risk muscle tension and ligament, tendon and joint overloading and pain.

5.3 Running – A Sport with a High Energy Demand

From a historical point of view, running is the most significant form of physical activity. Running races formed the centerpiece of the ancient Games (Olympics) and were at the heart of the revival of the Olympic ideal in the year 1896. Interest in running has been growing steadily since the 1980s. In the 1980 Berlin Marathon, only 363 runners took part, in 1985 there were 11,814, in 1990 25,000 and in 2005, there were 31,619.

Long distance running is now the most popular and most widespread endurance sport. For millions of runners, it is also the most beautiful sport. Fascinated by the feeling of freedom, and being motivated in all kinds of weather, countless miles are run every day around the world. Many people run to improve their fitness and health. They appreciate the comforting feeling of relaxation that they get from running. They love the challenge, the adventure and the excitement of racing.

Running is one of the highest energy-consuming forms of locomotion. You would have to cycle for twice as long to obtain the same effect. Running enables you to lose weight relatively easily, but it is not for everyone. It is extremely difficult to get started if you lack conditioning.

In the case of orthopedic problems or obesity (BMI > 30), alternative forms of cardiovascular exercise are recommended. In every running stride, you must absorb your bodyweight with your own strength, even when the muscles are already very tired. The natural muscular shock absorption reduces with fatigue and the impact is multiplied. [43]. If you are not in such good shape, you should initially raise your general trainability and fitness with low-impact sports, such as cycling, cross-country skiing or inline skating. The maximal force on the support and locomotor systems is substantially lower in these sports, thus avoiding overloading of the ligament and support tissue structures.

Running Technique

Despite the apparent simplicity of the movement technique, a good running technique is not that natural. The difference between runners is immense. Every running style leads to other loads on the locomotor system. Special **running training** makes sense in order to develop running optimally adapted to one's own requirements. Running technique is influenced by terrain, running surface and pace – foot placement, stride length and rate must all be variable to cope with these differences. Even the best running shoes cannot completely correct gait deficit or bring the foot into a "normal position" – their task is rather to support individual running styles. The best shoe does not replace active measures, such as the strengthening of the foot and leg muscles, foot gymnastics and running coordination drills.

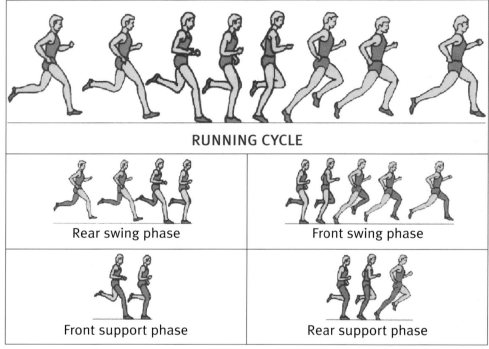

RUNNING CYCLE

Rear swing phase | Front swing phase

Front support phase | Rear support phase

Fig. 1/5.3: Running cycle

Tips for a relaxed and healthy running technique

- Strong **trunk muscles** are better at stabilizing the swinging action of the arms and legs. Weak trunk muscles cause the hips to tip forward, with a negative effect on hip extension and the push-off in the rear support phase, which can cause back problems.

- A relaxed **upper body** will enable you to support the running rhythm. Ideally you should lean slightly forward with your head upright looking at the ground about 10 yards in front of you.

- Relax your **hands** and bend your **arms** at the elbows at about 90° so that they swing loosely past the body. Well-coordinated arms and shoulders reduce the rotation about the body's longitudinal axis.

From Jogging to Racing

The word jogging means "moving slowly." Nearly every beginner makes the mistake of thinking that running must always be faster than walking. The difference between running and walking is in the technique, not the speed.

In walking, there is always one foot touching the ground, while running always features a flight phase. At the start, it is not a question of running as fast as possible. Your goal should be to go for as long as possible at a speed adapted to your individual ability – or to jog.

Running too fast not only leads to premature exhaustion but also means that you will not attain the desired feel-good factor. The flow experience, an easy-going, pleasant running sensation, only occurs when the demand is in line with one's own capabilities [56]. This requires an optimal load intensity, which can be determined using a heart rate monitor with OwnZone® function.

In the first 6-8 weeks, beginners should jog in the OwnZone Light, or 60-70% of HRmax. It is advisable to do 2-3 45-minute workouts per week, even if you have to intersperse with a few walking phases. After about 8 weeks, you will be able to run for 30-45 minutes without walking at all. From then on, you will enjoy running more and more.

The desire to run long distances grows automatically, so you should then increase your running time to about 60 minutes. Only after this is it advisable to increase the running speed and do a workout in the OwnZone® Hard, or at about 85% of HRmax.

5.4 Cycling – A Suitable Sport for Fat Metabolism Training

Cycling is the ideal sport for stimulating fat metabolism. Even untrained, overweight and seniors can efficiently train their fat metabolism from the very first workout, as long as the training surface is flat, they use a suitable bike and are able to ride it. This is almost impossible in any other endurance sport, as the prerequisite for effective fat metabolism training is long load times (> 60 minutes) at low intensity. In running, the intensity for beginners is usually too high or the low trainability of the support and locomotor systems means that the workout duration is limited. It should be noted here that fat metabolism training is not about losing weight or breaking down fat, but about increasing aerobic ability based on burning fat (betaoxidation of fatty acids). To achieve this, the exercise intensity should be in the OwnZone® Light or at 60-70% of HRmax. Untrained individuals should perform 2 or 3 60-90-minute workouts for at least four weeks in this heart rate target zone. To avoid overloading the joints, you should stick to an average pedaling rate of 80-100 cycles per minute.

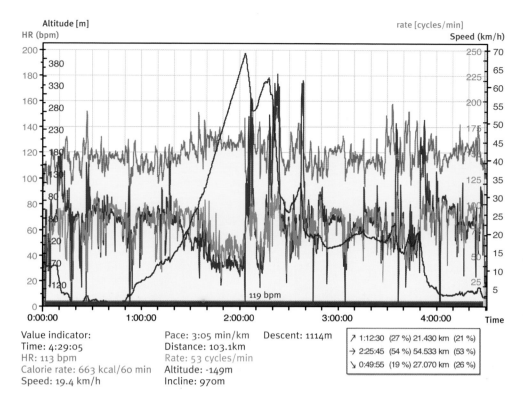

Value indicator:
Time: 4:29:05
HR: 113 bpm
Calorie rate: 663 kcal/60 min
Speed: 19.4 km/h

Pace: 3:05 min/km   Descent: 1114m
Distance: 103.1km
Rate: 53 cycles/min
Altitude: -149m
Incline: 970m

↗ 1:12:30 (27 %) 21.430 km (21 %)
→ 2:25:45 (54 %) 54.533 km (53 %)
↘ 0:49:55 (19 %) 27.070 km (26 %)

Fig. 1/5.4: HR, pedaling rate, speed and altimeter curves when cycling in the aerobic endurance zone (zone 2).

Endurance-trained athletes prefer the low intensity zone (60-70% HRmax) for long cycle rides (> 3 hours). Over short distances, the fat metabolism can also be trained at an intensity of 70-80% HRmax (OwnZone® Medium). For beginners and advanced, the last meal should be at least 2 hours before fat metabolism training and carbohydrate-rich drinks or bars should be avoided during cycling training itself. For long cycle rides (> 2 hours), the optimal sources of nutrition are: slightly sweetened drinks (6-8% sugar content), dry fruit and low carb bars consisting of fat, amino acids.

Cycling training is different in many ways from other types of endurance training. The athlete must work optimally with a piece of equipment. Frame size and geometry greatly influence the riding quality and determine the possible sitting position. A good bicycle frame is characterized by a high stiffness, low weight and aerodynamic construction. It must suit the rider's individual proportions (body to standover height).

DESIGNING A WORKOUT FOR DIFFERENT SPORTS

The **height of the saddle** can be calculated the following ways:

- Standover height (cm) x 0.66 for sporty mountain bikes

- Standover height (cm) x 0.66 minus 5-8cm for everyday and touring mountain bikes

- Standover height (cm) x 0.88-0.93 for racing bikes.

Partially or completely spring-mounted (full-suspension) bikes give a comfortable ride. The spring system should minimize the vibrations and impact load when riding, in order to reduce the strain on the support and locomotor system. Many cyclists report that a longer and more relaxed ride is possible with spring-mounted wheels. The difference between the height of the saddle and handlebars should be about 10cm.

There are plenty of tips in specialist cycling literature on how to establish the **optimal sitting position** on the bike. A good criterion for the saddle height is that with your legs straight, the heels can still touch the pedal in the bottom dead center. The hips should not slip over the sides of the saddle in the process. When you cycle, only the tips of your toes should rest on the pedal, so that the knee joint is not fully extended. The more accurately the sports bike is set up to suit the rider, the more efficiently the pedaling technique will be.

Safety pedals offer the best power transfer and facilitate a round pedaling action. In addition, they increase riding safety and save you from an unwanted, injury-causing slipping off the pedals. Watch out! First get used to this system on little-used, hazard-free terrain (e.g., in the parking lot of a shopping mall when it is quiet). The firm binding of shoe and pedal can only be loosened by twisting the foot to the side.

Seniors and all those who haven't ridden a bike for a while should take part in a **cycling safety course** with their own bike. Quick-reacting braking with the front and back wheel brakes, safe curve riding and controlled turning left and right in street traffic should be mastered. These are the preconditions for starting your first workout on the bike over a long distance without stopping. In cycling, the demand on the joints, tendons and ligaments is relatively low, even during workouts lasting several hours.

Optimizing the Pedaling Technique

The fact that every cyclist finds his own individual pedaling technique on the basis of what works best for him could make one question to what extent technique training is actually necessary. However, research into the pedaling techniques of experienced cyclists, triathletes and duathletes shows that even ambitious cyclists have inefficient

pedaling actions that neither they themselves nor the experienced eye of a coach can spot. Deviations from maximal power output and power development in the pedaling cycle between the right and left leg of over 10% are not uncommon. Asymmetries in the pedaling action can be caused by injuries and in the long term lead to muscular disbalances.

The modern pedaling technique is based on objective biofeedback monitoring. There are several systems available for practical use. Professional cyclists install a special power meter between the bottom bracket and the chain wheel. The performance (torque) is measured using a strain gauge. This not only allows the identification of asymmetries between right and left legs, but also the graph provides additional information about the power used in the individual movement phases. Polar Electro's power output system calculates the power and performance when pedaling over a power sensor and another sensor for chain velocity. The data are simultaneously sent to the digital wrist unit along with the heart rate, altitude and temperature measurements, where they are then stored. During the cycle ride, the power and output data can be displayed on the wrist unit (fig. 2-4/5.4).

DESIGNING A WORKOUT FOR DIFFERENT SPORTS

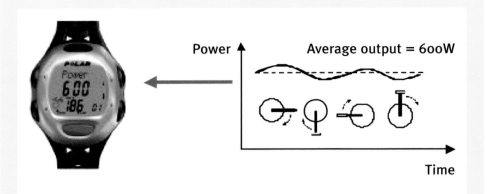

Fig. 2/5.4: Power meter: average performance from the last pedal rotation

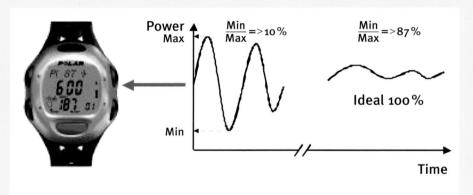

Fig. 3/5.4: Pedaling index: behavior of maximal and minimal performance during a crank rotation

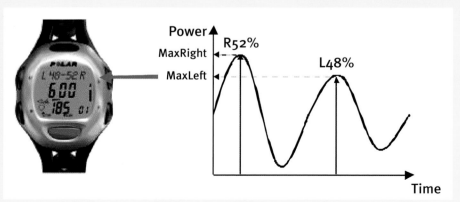

Fig. 4/5.4: Left-right balance: left and right leg output percentage

Technique Training with Biofeedback

Biofeedback on bilateral power output can help to achieve a "round" pedaling cycle. If deficiencies are diagnosed, they must be corrected by specific technique training, which involves incorporating a variety of exercise forms into the cycling workout. When you start technique training, you need to break your habitual pedaling rhythm by using different pedaling rates and emphasizing individual phases (e.g., focusing on pulling). Other methods are one-sided pedaling with extremely low pedaling rate and high resistance (lateral chain) and high pedaling rate and low resistance (medial chain).

All exercise forms use the interval method, i.e., alternate effort and rest. The aim is to improve proprioception. This special exercise program should last for about 15-30 minutes, after the warm-up phase, and should be carried out for several weeks. In a second phase of technique training, the technique variations are continuously reduced and the duration of the exercises increases. The aim is eventually to find an optimal individual pedaling rate, which gives the cyclist the feeling of a smooth, fluid and economical pedaling action. The success of the technique training can be measured by an improved right-left balance and a higher average cycling power output.

5.5 Swimming – A Good Compensation Sport

The fact that swimming involves movement in a different medium, water, makes it special. The specific gravity of the body is lower in water than on land. The body in water is almost "weightless." This leads to a beneficial **offloading of the support and locomotor system**, while at the same time protecting bones, joints, ligaments and tendons. The high resistance of water, even at low movement speeds, leads to higher demands on the muscles, cardiovascular and breathing systems. This makes swimming a particularly suitable sport for the overweight, those with back problems and degenerative joint conditions (arthritis).

Many athletes swim for regeneration and compensation. Swimming is an ideal post-competition compensation activity: it relaxes the muscles and promotes recovery. Swimming toughens the body up by strengthening the immune system. The calorie consumption when swimming is relatively high due to increased thermoregulation activity.

Swimming is not only a compensation sport. Someone who has learned several swimming strokes can definitely improve his fitness with a varied swimming program.

Heart rate measurement in swimming makes complete sense. Experience shows that occasional swimmers usually do not push themselves hard enough. The heart rate monitor has a motivating effect, especially if the calorie expenditure is displayed. Competitive swimmers use heart rate monitors to optimize the rests between intervals and to monitor the intensity during aerobic endurance training.

5.6 Cross-country Skiing – A Varied Form of Total Body Training

Very early on in the history of humanity, arduous surroundings led to the development of equipment that enabled people to move about on the snow [26]. Today, cross-country skiing is a popular sporty and recreational activity, a useful cross-training method for runners, cyclists, swimmers and a very interesting competitive sport with individual and mass starts, sprints, pursuit and the skiduathlon, in which both the classic and skating events follow each other without a break. The rediscovery, further development and firm establishment of skating technique in the 1980s and the technical innovations in cross-country skiing equipment have contributed significantly to the increasing attraction of cross-country ski sports.

The knowledge that varied training and the use of different training methods improve performance and help to prevent injuries is becoming more and more prevalent. From many points of view, cross-country skiing is a suitable training method for: basic endurance, movement coordination, and the training of the shoulder girdle and trunk muscles. Cross-country skiing provides an enjoyable feeling for movement in order to react to the constantly changing conditions, e.g., changing snow quality, the profile and condition of the trail.

Easy-to-Learn Basic Technique

A salient feature of the cross-country skiing technique is the diagonal coordination of arms and legs, which is also a basic requirement for an efficient technique in Nordic walking. If you have previous experience of this, the diagonal stride in cross-country is usually easy to learn. After a few hours of practice, long workouts can be performed to develop basic endurance ability.

All-Around, Gentle Total Body Training

The skis are moved forward by the coordinated use of the arms and legs. Different techniques are used for skiing in very uneven terrain. The skating techniques are particularly exciting. Every technique uses different muscle groups, so that after a workout nearly all the muscles have been trained. In no other sport do the muscles get such a varied, all-around workout. Boredom is never an issue. The continual changing of technique means that the muscle demand is not one-sided, local muscle fatigue is avoided and muscular balance is achieved. Cross-country skiing is a low-impact sport, and there are no high pressure loads, as there are in running. The gentle gliding along down the trail is easy on the support and locomotor system.

Training Intensity and Volume

The low-impact, total body training afforded by the sport allows training volumes that far exceed those of running alone. The pre-conditions for efficient fat metabolism and basic endurance training are therefore in place. Training is mainly done according to the endurance and fartlek methods at low and moderate intensity, i.e., in the OwnZone® Medium. While sport skating over an eneven course, intensity zones of 80-90% of HRmax or OwnZone® Hard can even be reached. This intensive type of training should not be done more than twice a week for a total of 90 minutes.

Ski Models for Different Needs and Target Groups

The categories of ski available have completely changed in the past few years (fig. 1/5.6). There is now a ski for every kind of skiing experience. The quality of the skis has also improved, not just for competitive skiing but also for recreational, adventure and experience sport. The equipment is both lighter and more robust, the gliding and quality of the ski has been improved and they have become shorter overall. The correct equipment guarantees more fun, an energy-saving run and a light, safe slide. The ski manufacturer Fischer offers an innovative range of skis for different target groups and ski experiences, for example.

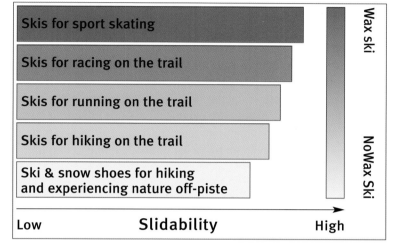

Fig. 1/5.6:
Ski models for different target groups [26]

Skis for sport skating

Skis for racing on the trail

Skis for running on the trail

Skis for hiking on the trail

Ski & snow shoes for hiking and experiencing nature off-piste

Low   Slidability   High

Wax ski

NoWax Ski

Skis for Adventure and Nature Experience

The skis should be wide, robust and light, and have good climbing properties. Skis with steel edges also give increased control in difficult terrain. The shoe should be breathable, well-padded and comfortable and the boot should reach at least ankle height. Modern equipment fulfills these requirements. In ski mountain tours off-piste, a special shoe with additional heel binding is necessary. This ensures your enjoyment of downhill alpine skiing, although you can still enjoy downhill skiing with the telemark technique.

Trail Touring Skis

Trail touring is suitable for everyone and requires no special technique. The natural, diagonal movement is transferred to the skis and poles. For trail touring, a NoWax ski of average width suitable for your bodyweight and height with a built-in climbing system. The demands on the shoe are comparable to those in off-piste terrain.

Nordic Cruising Skis

For Nordic trail cruising, you can choose between wax skis and NoWax skis. The wax ski has a completely smooth surface of which the slide quality can be improved by glide waxing the gliding zone with glide wax and the push-off zone with easy grip wax. The bottom of NoWax skis has a special structured coating that provides the necessary resistance to the bottom of the skis. This is why wax is not necessary. Structures like scales, crown tec, microscales or chemical coatings provide a certain glide resistance in the direction of movement and give the required grip. Nordic Cruising skis have a double hourglass shape and are wider under foot and at the tip. This gives a wider but shorter surface in contact with the snow for an overall shorter ski length.

Recreational skis have become lighter due to the use of high-quality materials, the blade has become more robust and the surface more adaptable to changing external conditions.

The Classic Ski for Racing Skiers

The sport ski is a wax ski, individually prepared for skiing technique and external conditions. The classic cross-country ski technique can be learned perfectly with the wax ski. The ski should be light and have an optimal ratio between length and tension for optimal glide and push-off quality. The choice of ski tension depends on the skier's push-off power and technique, his bodyweight and the type of skiing (competitive or leisure). Ski tension can be established using the paper test.

Skis for Ski Skating

The skating ski has a continuous gliding surface, is shorter and has a higher tension and stiffness than the classic ski. With the use of special technology from the aviation construction industry and the changed composition of the skis, skating skis are now very light. The optimized mass distribution (lower weight at the front and back) minimizes the inertia of the skis and returns them more quickly to the ideal push-off position after every stride.

The newest models also have a double hourglass shape. These skis have better glide and push-off qualities. This waisting in the front and rear of the ski makes it easier to push during the pushing phase and distributes the push more evenly over the whole ski edge.

The waisting also improves the glide and control of the skis. The reinforcing of the substructure of the ski further optimizes the power transfer and provides a high lateral and torsion stability.

Cross-country Ski Shoes

When purchasing cross-country ski shoes, you should look for a comfort and a good fit. Good shoes are breathable and waterproof and have special soles that insulate against the cold. Cross-country skis have different insole hardness (soft, medium and stiff).

Soft soles are recommended for classic running and touring, and hard soles are more suitable for ski skating. The **skating shoe** has a higher cut and looks similar to a mountain boot. The sole is relatively hard and stiff.

Cross-country Ski Poles

Ski poles should be unbreakable, stable and light. Nowadays, cross-country skiers prefer poles made of carbon, carbon fiber or light metals (e.g., aluminum). Use the following rule to determine the correct pole length: poles for classic technique should be no more than shoulder-height and skating ski poles should reach the tip of your nose.

Pole length varies according to individual skiing technique and arm strength, which is why competitive skiers usually choose longer skis than recreational skiers. Short poles are necessary for short sprinting distances to allow faster speed of movement.

5.7 Inline Skating – A Demanding Sport

Inline skating is a lifetime sport that is ideal for the young and old alike. Skating is not only fun, but develops lasting overall fitness. Endurance, strength and coordination are trained with no high pressure loading.

You can perform countless moves and figures on inline skates that are exciting for both children and adults. The variety knows no bounds. It is up to each individual to decide what works for them, which requires an objective evaluation of your own ability.

Assessing Your Fitness and Ability Correctly

Many people forget that they haven't exercised for years and tend to overestimate their ability. It is not easy to move around safely on skates. The skating technique requires coordination and a feeling for movement, which cannot be taken for granted if you have many years of physical inactivity.

The muscles have "forgotten" how to react appropriately to new movement stimuli. Movements are uncoordinated and the sense of balance is reduced, rhythm is hard to find and reactions are slower. All these abilities are very important in skating.

Safety First – Never Skate without Protective Gear

The injury statistics for inline skating show that many beginners skate without sufficient road safety awareness and the necessary protective gear. Typical injuries like grazes, bruises, twists, sprains and head injuries can be avoided or significantly reduced by wearing a helmet and knee, elbow and wrist guards and by undergoing intensive technical training. Apart from bothersome scars, frequent trivial injuries like light grazes and bruises can lead to cartilage damage in the long term.

Learn How to Fall – Fall without Getting Hurt

The main reasons for falls are an over upright body posture, inadequate skating technique, slow reactions, lack of conditioning, over-estimating your own ability and doing silly things. The seriousness of the fall injuries varies. Skaters who have repeatedly practiced how to fall and who wear adequate protective gear usually come out of falls unscathed.

Warming up Increases Safety

Warming up before skating raises the body temperature, which enables the muscles to perform better. Movements are more fluid, perception and reactions are better and the risk of falling decreases. The warm-up should consist of at least five minutes of jogging and then stretching the main muscle groups (see chapter 5.1).

The "Right" Intensity

When skating, choose a speed that suits your technical level. You can monitor the intensity by measuring your heart rate. A healthy, preventive, valuable and performance-enhancing load is 60-80% of your HRmax. Start off by training in the OwnZone® Light, i.e., at 60-70% of HRmax. Increase the workout duration in the first weeks from 30 minutes initially to more than 90 minutes. The longer you skate at a moderate pace, the more effectively you stimulate the fat metabolism.

Inline Skating Develops Muscle Balance

Inline skating trains and uses muscle groups that are neglected during most everyday activities and in the training for many sports. Muscular disbalances are known to be the cause of many locomotor system problems. For example, skating is great for strengthening the back muscles, the front shin muscle, the adductors, the quadriceps and the calf muscles.

What Can Be Done about Back Problems?

Pain in your back muscles can spoil your enjoyment of skating. The pain is usually felt when you lean forward, causing the back muscles have to work very hard. Depending on your fitness, the muscles can even get tired after a few minutes, after which they can no longer fulfill their stabilizing and holding function. The pressure loading on the spine in the lower back (transition to the sacrum) is greatly increased, resulting in back pain. Straightening up and stretching your back regularly can relieve this pain.

Beginners can also experience back pain when skating upright. This is mainly due to weak back muscles and insufficient dynamic balancing ability, which cause muscular tension and relatively unsteady movement with partially uncontrolled wobbling movements. To prevent back pain, to begin with you should only skate for short stretches and have regular breaks. You should focus on training the coordination and strength of your back and pelvis stabilizing muscles without skates beforehand.

6 TRAINING FOR DIFFERENT TARGET GROUPS

6.1 The Untrained, Healthy Beginner

It is never too late to start moderate fitness training. As coordination and conditioning are lifelong trainable qualities, sports training even until a very old age leads to a noticeable improvement in physical performance.

It is true that exercise cannot stop the aging process, but fitness and ability can be maintained for longer – you can be 40 for 20 years! Moderate exercise can make this possible.

If you have not done any exercise for years, you should not immediately go out with the idea that "more is more." This can overload your muscles, ligaments, tendons and joints and actually limit your progress. You would also miss out on the recreational and fun aspect of exercise and the pleasant feeling of relaxation it brings.

Don't look too much at what others are doing, just concentrate on yourself and on your own needs and ability. The biggest mistake that you can make when you take up a sport is to put yourself under pressure.

Incorporating fitness training into a habitual daily routine can be a big problem for many beginners. They must often rethink their priorities in order to be able to find time to exercise.

To make sure that you really make time for exercise, plan definite dates for it and try to arrange training together with your friends. Sport not only makes you more lively and fit; you will also be able to do things that you have not been able to do for years.

In order to meet the goals you have set yourself, you will need to find the right training volume and intensity. Not everyone is equally able to do a workout in the optimal intensity zone. Experiment and get to know your body. Your personal goal should be to work out 3 or 4 times per week for 60 minutes, burning 1,000-1,500 calories per week after 2-3 months.

Suitable Sports

Endurance sports are the most suitable introduction to sporting activity. Choose the sport that best corresponds to your personal preferences and inclinations, and that you find easiest to incorporate into your daily life. If you enjoy working out, it will be easier for you to do it. Your existing physical condition is also important when you choose your sport. Overweight individuals, or those with orthopedic problems, especially in the hip and knee joints, should go for low-impact sports like swimming, aquajogging, inline skating, walking and cycling, as they are easy on the joints. If your body is accustomed to aerobic exercise, even high-impact sports, like running, will not seem difficult.

Training Structure

The goal in the first 3-4 weeks is to do an aerobic cardiovascular workout 3 times per week for about 20-30 minutes. Rest for a day or two between workouts so that your body has time to adapt to the new stimuli. After 4-6 weeks, the training will already have a beneficial effect on your well-being. An objective sign of this is a lower resting heart rate. In order to make further progress, it is advisable to increase the workout duration very gradually to 60 minutes. After about 8 weeks, it is realistic to do endurance sports like Nordic walking, cycling, inline skating, etc., several times a week for 45-90 minutes. This weekly exercise program leads to an energy consumption of 1,500-2,000 calories and goes a long way to improving your health and well-being.

Effort and Intensity

It is sometimes hard to exercise at the right intensity. Many beginners start off by training too hard and have to reduce the pace because of lactic acid build-up in the muscles. Training like this does little to develop basic endurance because anaerobic (without oxygen) metabolism is activated too soon and it represses the aerobic metabolism (with oxygen).

To avoid this, you should monitor your exercise intensity with a heart rate monitor and always begin your workouts with a gentle warm-up lasting at least 5 minutes, during which the heart rate should not rise above 130 bpm for men or 140 bpm for women.

In the main part of your workout, you should train in target zone 3 between 70 and 85% of HRmax. Try to stay as near to the lower limit (70%) as possible. For beginners to be able to exercise for 20 minutes in this target zone, it may be necessary to add a few active rest breaks, like walking.

6.2 The Ambitious Fitness Athlete

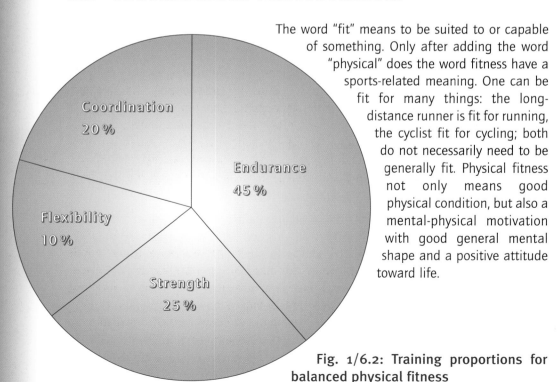

The word "fit" means to be suited to or capable of something. Only after adding the word "physical" does the word fitness have a sports-related meaning. One can be fit for many things: the long-distance runner is fit for running, the cyclist fit for cycling; both do not necessarily need to be generally fit. Physical fitness not only means good physical condition, but also a mental-physical motivation with good general mental shape and a positive attitude toward life.

Coordination 20%

Endurance 45%

Flexibility 10%

Strength 25%

Fig. 1/6.2: Training proportions for balanced physical fitness

Physical fitness is composed of endurance, strength, speed, flexibility and coordination. From middle age onwards, the speed component becomes less important. The proportions of each quality in the development of physical fitness are different at different times of our lives. The training proportions shown in fig. 1/6.2 shift in the senior years (> 65 years) to a stronger emphasis on coordination and strength training.

Flexibility Training: Flexibility is the ability to carry out movements within the possible range of motion of the joints. There are two types of flexibility: active-dynamic, i.e., the ability to attain an optimal range of motion (flexion, extension) with low stretching resistance during movement, and passive-dynamic, in which a maximal range of motion is achieved by exerting a passive external force. Flexibility depends on the structure and properties of the muscle-tendon tissue (elasticity, plasticity, viscosity) and decreases with age and also increased muscle cross-section, muscular fatigue and cold. Tendons and muscles with little stretchability limit mobility and therefore performance levels.

The combination of low muscle strength and poor stretchability of muscles and tendons is the most frequent cause of injury and pain in the muscle-tendon-ligament structure.

Coordination Training (sensorimotor training)**:** Coordination is the ability to control a single or complex movement in terms of time, space and strength. Coordinative abilities are important in all movements and form the basis for the acquisition of good movement technique in sports. It can decide the success and failure of a movement action. Coordinative abilities include balance, sense of rhythm, kinesthetic differentiation ability, adaptation ability, linking ability and spatial orientation ability. Targeted training and exercise forms are necessary to retain good movement coordination well into the senior years.

Strength Training: Strength is the ability to overcome resistance using muscle activity, i.e., to lift weights (concentric muscle contraction); to work against them, e.g., to jump down from something (eccentric muscle contraction); and to stop something (isometric muscle contraction). The primary goal of muscle training for fitness purposes is to ensure a functional posture and movement stability during long-lasting or repeated physical exercise. For training, this means concentrating on exercises for the general strengthening of the core muscles of the trunk (back and abdominals) and the shoulder and pelvic girdle.

Endurance Training: Endurance is the ability to cope with a continuous demand on the body and to delay the loss of performance due to fatigue. Endurance improves when the endurance activities (Nordic walking, running, cycling, etc.) are carried out for several weeks at a moderate intensity and for a duration of at least 30 minutes per workout. In chapters 5.2 to 5.7, you can find various tips on training for the classic endurance disciplines of (Nordic) walking, running, cycling, swimming, cross-country skiing and inline skating.

A balanced, varied fitness program includes endurance training in different sports for cardio-pulmonary fitness, strength training on machines for all the large muscle groups, a strengthening program for the core trunk muscles, gymnastic

exercises for more flexibility and coordination training for stability and movement confidence. Physical fitness is developed extensively in ball games: streetball, beach volleyball or football, which not only provide fun and variety, but also develop conditioning and coordination.

Of course you cannot train everything at once. You have to set priorities throughout the year. Holiday periods, weather conditions and personal preferences determine the type and volume of the activity and allow no place for boredom and monotony. The ambitious fitness athlete exercises nearly every day.

6.3 **The Competitive Athlete**

While recreational athletes practice different sports and use a variety of training methods in order to acquire general physical fitness, competitive athletes strive for maximal performance in one sport. To achieve this, they not only practice their chosen sport but supplement their sport-specific training with other training methods in order to achieve a higher general trainability, gain muscular balance, prevent overloading and promote regeneration and compensation by doing light exercise (RECOM Training).

However, supplementary sports should not just be selected and sequenced at random. This would reduce the efficiency of the training and lead to pain and injury and possibly jeopardize performance improvement in the primary sport. Instead, the training must be sensibly structured according to the principles of training methodology and exercise physiology. The commonalities and differences of the coordinative and conditioning factors, and the demand they place on the support and locomotor systems, should be considered for every training method.

The proportion of general training decreases throughout a several-year training plan and also during the training year. In the general preparation period, the competitive athlete should be doing about 20-30% of his training using non-specific methods. For instance, the runner not only concentrates on running but also does cycling, inline skating, swimming, cross-country skiing or strength training.

Training Volume

The training volume of a competitive athlete is on average 8-15 hours per week. For a long-distance runner, this means a weekly mileage of 50-80 miles. This gives an annual total of about 2,000-2,500 miles (tab. 1/6.3). 70-75% of this total is done in the basic endurance zone, 10-15% in the aerobic endurance zone, 5-10% in the anaerobic threshold zone and 3-5% in the red line zone.

Tab. 1/6.3:
Training volume in therapeutic, recreational, competitive and elite sport

	Weekly total training hours	Weekly running hours	Weekly running mileage	Annual running mileage
Therapeutic sports	3-4	2-3	6-20	250-550
Fitness sports	4-7	3-5	20-40	650-1400
Competitive sports	8-15	6-10	50-80	2000-2500
Elite sports	10-20	8-14	80-175	3000-5000

Avoiding Training Errors

We usually start to look for training errors when our performance level stagnates or drops. The causes are usually complex. A detailed training diary is needed to solve the problem. Experience shows that many athletes make the same mistakes, which are listed on the next page.

1. The training intensity is too high in the basic endurance zone.

2. The proportion of training in each zone is wrong. Usually the volume in the intensive workouts (anaerobic threshold, VO_2max) is too high and too low in the extensive workouts (aerobic endurance).

3. The training plan is not sufficiently adapted to suit the individual's ability and trainability. Beginners often train too intensively and too often.

4. The training load does not increase during the year; it is higher in the general preparation period than in the special preparation period.

5. The endurance training is too monotonous, i.e., standard distances, same distance profile, same training method and same intensity.

6. The work:rest cycle is not respected, leading to incomplete adaptation and a drop in training quality due to fatigue.

7. The loading peaks in training are too close together (less than two weeks) or too far apart (more than two months).

8. The mental preparation for competition is inadequate. Psychological methods of competition preparation are not used.

9. The post-competition regeneration phase is too short. Competitions are done without compensation training in between.

10. Training continues unreduced at the first signs of sickness (e.g., a coming infection) or nagging pain in the support and locomotor system, instead of immediately taking the necessary measures (reducing training, regeneration, seeing a physician, etc.)

Have Regular Health Checks
if Your Performance Requirements Are High

Qualified sports medical care is essential for all competitive sporting activity, as are regular check-ups. This is especially true for ambitious beginners or returners over the age of 40. Even if you have an annual health visit, you must take responsibility for monitoring your day-to-day health. The medical check-up is not an annual guarantee of good health. The athlete must always be sensitive to his body's reactions during and after working out and adapt his training accordingly. Every training plan must be immediately adapted to changing performance conditions.

6.4 The Overweight

Overweight means 10-25% heavier than normal weight. **Obesity** is defined as an excess of body fat [49]. The basic calculation for the weight classification is the body mass index (BMI). The BMI is the quotient of weight and height squared.

Tab. 1/6.4: BMI classification of body weight for adults

BMI (Body-Mass-Index) in kg/m^2	Classification
BMI below 18.5	Underweight
BMI 18.5-24.9	Normal weight
BMI 25-29.9	Overweight – requiring treatment in combination with other risk factors, such as high blood pressure, diabetes, elevated blood lipids, etc.
BMI 30-34.9	Obese I – requiring treatment without other risk factors
BMI 35-39.9	Obese II – also requiring treatment without other risk factors
BMI > 40	Obese III – high health risk!

In Germany, according to a study by the Federal Statistics Office (April 2004) [65], about 29% of women and 44% of men are overweight. 14% of men and 12% of women are obese.

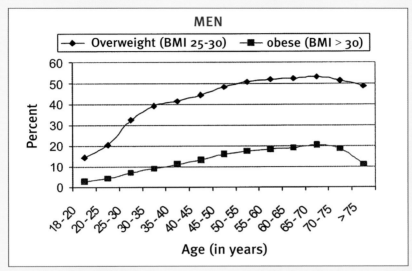

Fig. 1/6.4:
Proportion of obese and overweight men in Germany [65]

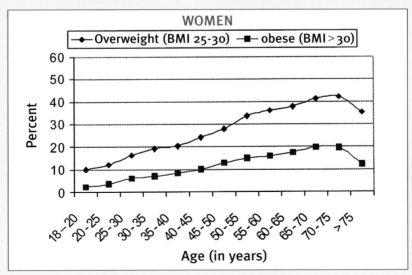

Fig. 2/6.4:
Proportion of obese and overweight women in Germany [65]

Evaluation of Body Weight

Calculation of the BMI alone is not enough to evaluate your bodyweight, as it does not distinguish between men and women and does not account for the body composition ratio (e.g., the proportion of non-fat mass to total body mass).

There are a few ways of determining body composition. The most accurate, but also the one that requires most time and equipment, is underwater weighing and computer tomography. A cheaper and easier method for anyone to do is a skin fold measurement or a bioimpedance measurement.

Bioelectric Impedance Measurement

This method is based on the conductibility of the electric current through the body. While a very weak electric current (500-800 μA at 50 kHz) is sent through the body, the electrical resistance of the body tissue is measured. The body fat percentage is then calculated by taking gender, bodyweight and height into account. The results vary during the day due to changing water balance and slight changes in body temperature. The electrical resistance is therefore somewhat lowered after exercise when the body temperature is raised and there is improved blood circulation and increased water content of the muscle tissue.

Skin Fold Measurement

Special calipers are used to measure the thickness of the skin fold with the underlying fat tissue at certain points on the body. These separate values are then used to calculate the body fat percentage.

The Importance of Fat Distribution for the Health

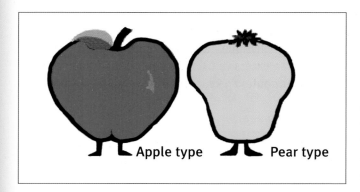

Apple type   Pear type

Fat is an important source of energy for the body. However, nowadays the average consumption is much too high. If more energy in the form of fats or carbohydrates is consumed than needed, the surplus energy is stored in fat deposits.

The location of the fat deposits on the body is important in determining the health risks of being overweight. Body fat distribution can be calculated from the quotient of waist and hip circumference. In men, if the quotient is more than 1, and greater than 0.85 in women, it corresponds to a central fat distribution pattern or "apple type." A lower quotient corresponds to a peripheral fat distribution or "pear type," which has lower risks [47].

For the pear type, the excess fat is located primarily around the thighs and bottom. The apple type, which is typical of men, is characterized by increased fat storage around the stomach. This raises the risk of cardiovascular illness and diabetes more than in the case of the pear type fat distribution. Distribution patterns are partly genetically conditioned and gender-specific.

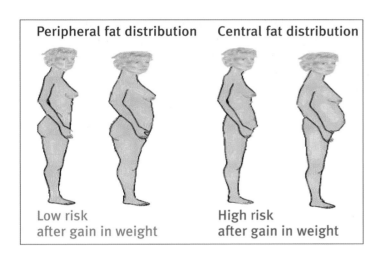

Peripheral fat distribution   Central fat distribution

Low risk
after gain in weight

High risk
after gain in weight

Fig. 3/6.4:
Peripheral and central weight distribution before and after weight gain

Causes of Overweight and Obesity

There are many factors that give rise to being overweight or obese. They can be due to individual, societal or socio-cultural events and influences. Lack of self-esteem, personal frustration, misguided ideas about ideal physique, acquired eating habits and inadequate conflict resolution can lead to an excessive calorie intake. In addition, lack of exercise and a high-calorie diet also contribute. The superfluous calories are stored in the form of fat.

Lack of exercise, whether in the gym or just in daily activities, reinforces the hypercalorific energy balance. With the exceptions of illness or constitutional factors, we can actively influence all other factors that cause obesity.

The Health Consequences of Being Overweight

Being overweight represents an enormous load for all the organs and particularly for the heart. It favors the appearance of other risk factors like high blood pressure, elevated blood lipids and diabetes. Body mass indices of > 30 significantly increase the danger of cardiovascular diseases (heart attack, stroke, etc.). In order to reduce these health risks, a permanent change in lifestyle is essential.

What are the Effects of a 20 lb Weight Loss?

- Death from diabetes: reduced by 30%

- Cancer caused by being overweight: reduced by 40%

- Total mortality rate: reduced by 20%

- Total cholesterol: reduced by 10%

- Systolic resting blood pressure: reduced by 10 mm Hg.

Weight Management by Exercise, Nutrition and Lifestyle Modification

You should have a basic weight-loss program that encompasses modifications of exercise, nutrition and lifestyle.

Lifestyle Changes
It is important that you set realistic goals and aim for a weight loss that can actually be achieved in a particular time frame, e.g., losing 4 lb in a month.

Unrealistic goals make it too easy to return to former bad habits. Even if you don't reach your ideal weight, any distinct weight loss is a good personal achievement that will have positive effects on your health and self-confidence.

You should be fully convinced of the benefits of lasting changes in nutrition and exercise habits, as otherwise you will not be able to keep them going in the long term. Give yourself time, as fat that has accumulated over months and years is not going to disappear overnight. It is similar to giving up smoking, in that support from friends and family is very beneficial and helps to prevent relapses.

Modified Nutrition

You lose weight if you consume less energy than you use, but it is hard to change the habits of a lifetime. It is helpful to analyze your eating and drinking habits with a diet log in order to be able to spot possible reasons for the increased energy consumption. There are no miracle diets that enable you to drop huge amounts in a few days, or even to lose weight overnight. On the contrary, they hide the danger of the so-called "yo-yo effect." That means that after a short time, your weight will return to its starting point and perhaps be even higher.

The German Nutrition Society recommends a balanced, mixed diet to lose weight, which is low in fat, high in carbohydrates, rich in fiber and contains no more than 1,200-1,500 kcal/day. A daily consumption of fewer than 1,000 calories is usually not enough to provide a balanced diet, and deficiency symptoms like protein breakdown can occur in the muscles. In combination with increased exercise and a modified lifestyle, this diet enables an average weight loss of about 0.6-2 lb per week.

Exercise

A changed diet combined with an ongoing exercise program brings long-term improvements to your body composition. With regular exercise, you can maintain or even reduce your bodyweight without changing your eating habits.

Untrained individuals should gradually increase their metabolic rate weekly by physical activity.

One Step at a Time

The first step toward more exercise and physical fitness starts in everyday life. Avoid the elevator and use the stairs instead, leave your car at home and cycle instead, if you can.

The next step is to do 30 minutes of exercise 2 or 3 times per week. You should burn at least 150 kcal per workout. The weekly calorie consumption during exercise should be at least 1,000 kcal. After about 4 weeks, increase the calorie expenditure to at least 300 kcal per workout.

The weekly calorie expenditure in exercise should be 1,500-2,000 kcal. The longer the training duration, the more effective the fat burning effect. The amount of fat burned increases in the case of an average endurance trained individual from 30% in the first 15 minutes to more than 40% after about 45 minutes.

The Right Intensity

It is easy to determine your optimal exercise intensity accurately using a heart rate monitor. With the OwnZone® function (see chapter 3.5), you can determine your individual training heart rate based on your current physical condition.

If you want to achieve a long-term weight loss, an exercise intensity for endurance training of 60-75% of HRmax is ideal. You can calculate this zone with the OwnZone® Weight or Light. If you want to improve your fitness, as well as losing weight, the intensity zone of 65-75% of HRmax would be the right choice. This corresponds to OwnZone® Basic.

- **OwnZone® Weight/Light (about 60-76% of HRmax):** The ideal training zone for weight management (activating the fat metabolism).

- **OwnZone® Basic (about 65-85% of HRmax):** The ideal training zone for weight maintenance and to improve cardiovascular fitness for experienced athletes.

Aerobic endurance training helps your body accumulate enzymes that break down fat and turn you into a long-term fatburner. Beginners need to be patient until their metabolism adapts to the unfamiliar demands placed on it. The total calorie expenditure is of course greater during intensive training due to the higher carbohydrate proportion. However, in the long term, intensive training stops your metabolism from burning more fat at rest.

Suitable Sports

For the overweight, low-impact sports like (Nordic) walking, cross-country skiing, cycling and swimming are a good choice. These sports do not unduly overload your bones, joints and ligaments. Chose a sport that you enjoy, perhaps that you can do with others and that you can easily incorporate into your daily routine several times a week.

(Nordic) Walking

Jogging is difficult for very overweight people. It is better and more motivating to try a less intensive low-impact sport. Walking has the advantages of an endurance sport and is more suitable for overweight people or those with joint damage or following hip replacement than jogging, as the pressure load is much lower.

Cycling

Cycling is especially good for the overweight, as the bodyweight is supported by the saddle. Ergometer bike training is also quite suitable. The desired load can be accurately determined and programmed. Compared to jogging or walking, it does have the disadvantage that the muscle mass used is lower and the local application of force required is greater.

Swimming

In the water, you feel buoyant, you only need to support a small percentage of your own body mass. The water also hides excess body mass. In aquajogging, you wear a buoyancy belt so that you can jog in deep water. The sport is extremely low-impact.

Weight Management with the Heart Rate Monitor

Special programs have been developed for some heart rate monitors that are intended to help you lose weight realistically and permanently. These programs rely on the combination of sensible nutrition and exercise and give individual advice for daily and weekly calorie requirements and expenditure.

The energy expenditure is measured with the OwnCal® function and based on the personal data (gender, age, bodyweight, training heart rate in relation to HRmax, VO_2max). The OwnCal® function shows the energy expenditure during and after a workout as well as the accumulated expenditure. The higher the heart rate, the lower the energy expenditure.

The energy consumption is entered using the buttons on the wrist unit, where it is processed. These two factors, calorie consumption and intake, are the deciding factors for the optimal energy balance. Only when energy expenditure is greater than energy consumption will you lose weight. An equal energy balance will ensure that your target weight is maintained.

6.5 Training with Reduced Cardiovascular Function

The human body is genetically predisposed to move. However, the modern sedentary lifestyle of "Homo Industrialis" does not suit our bodies' need for movement and causes health problems.

Despite improved medical care, cardiovascular diseases are among the most serious societal and medical problems of Western industrialized countries. This is mainly due to an increase in the prevalence of heart failure [40].

The main causes for this increase are longer life expectancy and an increase of epidemic proportions of Type II diabetes and obesity. These are in turn favored by a lack of exercise. There is a definite link between physical activity and cardiovascular disease.

Lack of exercise is an independent risk factor and this has been confirmed by the American Heart Association (AHA), the World Health Organization (WHO) and the International Sports Medicine Federation (FIMS). The German Cardiology Society also recommends regular exercise. However, 30% of Germans are hardly ever active, 45% do no sport and only 13% do the recommended amount of exercise (1,000 kcal per week).

For years, it was assumed that rest was essential in cases of heart disease. Meanwhile, numerous studies have shown that even diseased hearts are trainable. Regular exercise for people with reduced cardiovascular function is important and even necessary in order to encourage healing processes and to stabilize and restore physical performance.

However, there are still some established cardiologists who think that exercise is dangerous in the case of cardiovascular diseases.

But the risk of a sudden cardiac death, an acute cardio decompensation or a non-fatal heart attack during moderate physical activity is becoming lower and lower [19], as long as the training is adapted to the individual's changed conditions and not borrowed directly from fitness and recreational sport.

Preconditions for Cardiac Rehabilitation

Load control is the most important part of the training process and its effectiveness determines whether a training program is successful or not. Successful and low-risk exercise therefore requires accurate loading. Sport can only provide its greatest therapeutic and prophylactic benefits if exercise programs are tailored to the individual. A basic condition for optimal training program design for cardiac rehabilitation is that they are guided by the principles of medicine and sports science. That is why a performance diagnostic test is essential prior to participation in a cardiac rehabilitation program. This entails carrying out a stress ECG on a bike ergometer (fig. 1/6.5).

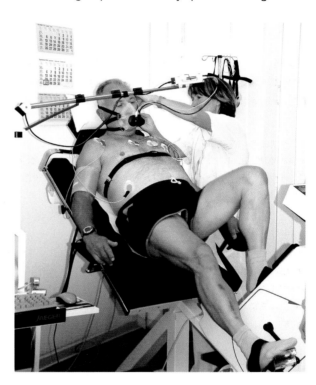

Fig. 1/6.5: Health check on a bike ergometer

The standard of the World Health Organization allows for a load increase of 25 Watts/2 minutes until maximal cardiac load or the limit indicated by the symptoms is reached. For every loading stage, the heart rate, blood pressure, lactate concentration and oxygen uptake are noted. The training heart rate is calculated on the basis of a complex analysis of the test data and the medical diagnosis. Merely measuring the heart rate is not enough in the case of cardiac patients, as the heart rate behavior can be influenced by medication.

To what extent a patient with reduced cardiovascular function may follow an exercise program is a matter for the doctor or cardiologist in charge. Contraindications for cardiac rehab are an unstable angina pectoris, a resting blood pressure > 200/110mmHg, a critical aortic stenosis, uncontroled arrhthmia, decompensated heart failure and an acute pericarditis or myocarditis [55]. If these conditions are present, participation in cardiac rehab represents an unmanageable risk.

What Should the Exercise Heart Rate Be?

Too often, exercise intensity is calculated according to rigid standard formulae (180 – age) and Watt formulae (25-50-75 Watt). Even the recommendations of international associations [4, 18, 53] are of little practical use. So, for exercise intensity guidelines ranging from 40-90% of HRmax, VO_2max or heart rate reserve (HRR) are made. From a sports science point of view, this is alarming. In the case of reduced cardiovascular function, the exercise intensity should not and cannot be calculated using such crude formulae. Heart diseases are complex, and are linked to individual case history and/or combined with various additional health problems, such as diabetes or obesity. This makes generalized and standardized recommendations difficult or even impossible.

Up to now, rehab has been done by the following method: the lower the physical performance level, the lower the exercise intensity. The relevant literature [7, 15] recommends aerobic, low-dose endurance training (< 50% of VO_2max) for patients with greatly reduced physical trainability. Exercising in this zone represents a low load for the left ventricle. Basically, the intensity guidelines must be calculated individually, using the still-available function reserves, in order to avoid over or underloading.

Endurance Training Design in Cardiac Rehab Programs

Endurance training is said to have an important preventive and rehabilitative effect, due to the varied and beneficial effects on the cardiovascular system. The aim is principally to improve cardiovascular performance, to lower myocardial oxygen consumption and blood pressure, and reduce elevated blood lipids (LDL cholesterol). Particularly light to moderate endurance training for a duration of 30 minutes boosts regeneration and general well-being, activates the metabolism and economizes and stabilizes the cardiovascular system.

The endurance method is not always suitable for cardiac patients though. Patients who have a VO_2max of less than 20 ml/min/kg should train primarily with the interval method. Interval training has proven to be particularly effective in cardiac rehab for patients with pronounced peripheral load intolerance and premature cardiac fatigue. In interval training, a two- to three-fold greater peripheral load can be reached compared to the endurance method [38, 39], and the cardiovascular stress drops significantly. The parameters that may be varied in interval training are interval length, rest structure and intensity.

(Nordic) walking, hiking, cycling and swimming are particularly recommended for endurance training in the secondary prevention of cardiovascular disease. **Nordic walking** and **trekking** are natural forms of locomotion and are ideal sports to start with [50]. The **bicycle** is also a suitable piece of training equipment. Especially when beginning regular training, bike ergometer training is a good choice.

Exercise intensity and training duration can be deliberately set and monitored. Once you have made a start, cycling in the open air is a great idea and offers substantially more variety. In your search for a suitable training route, you should look for one that is flat and protected from the wind. **Swimming** is especially suitable for people who also suffer from obesity and joint problems, for muscles, bones, joints and ligaments are moved gently and protected. The circulation is also activated by the movement, the water temperature and pressure. The recommended heart rate cannot be transferred directly from land to water.

Strength and Flexibility Training for Cardiac Rehabilitation

Up to now, endurance has been used in cardiac rehabilitation, but in order to be able to cope with everyday life (at work), endurance training alone is insufficient. Strength training has long been rejected in cardiac rehab and is contraindicated in the case of such problems as chronic heart failure. The negative image of strength training is due to data measured during isometric exercise that led to pathological changes in the peripheral resistance and to massive increases in blood pressure. However, current research results [38] show that the skeletal muscles have special importance as the organs that maintain a balance of catabolic and anabolic factors and, therefore, the regulation of the entire body.

For many cardiac patients enforced bed rest, physical inactivity and/or glucocortoid therapy led to an additional loss of muscle mass and strength.

Adequate strength training can compensate for this loss, while simultaneously improving cardiac efficiency.

The risk can be significantly reduced for cardiac patients when the strength training program is designed in line with the behavior of their blood pressure. The blood pressure is proportional to intensity, duration of the contraction and size of the muscles involved. Cardiac patients can either do strength training with machines or in the form of circuit training in the gym, using only their bodyweight, small weights or therabands. A dynamic strength endurance circuit consisting of 8-12 simple exercises for the large muscle groups has proved to be successful. The circuit should be done once or twice a week, and the number of reps (about 15-20) and rest structure must be adapted to individual ability.

The reactions of the cardiovascular system to targeted strength endurance training are not to be underestimated. Personal heart rate records have shown that with a targeted coordination of exercise duration and rest duration, an interval type demand on the cardiovascular system can be achieved (fig. 2/6.5) that is comparable to extensive interval training in endurance sport.

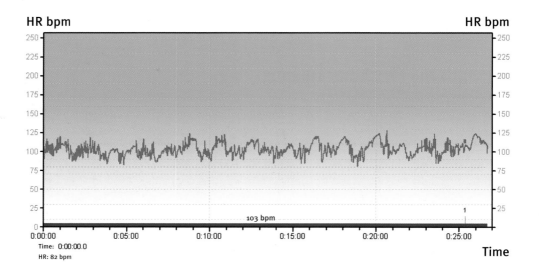

Fig. 2/6.5: Heart rate tachogram of a 58-year-old heart patient (EF*= 25%, HRmax = 143 min⁻¹ during strength endurance training (10 exercises)

Coordination Training in Cardiac Rehabilitation

Coordination is as important in cardiac rehab as strength training as a factor in the economy of movement and psychomotor activity. A primary goal of build-up and maintenance training for all kinds of special groups is the economy of movement. When a movement is done economically, i.e., the same movement is carried out with a lower energy expenditure, the demand is correspondingly lower on the cardiovascular system. Only the improvement of intermuscular coordination can lead to a performance increase of up to 10% [23]. For patients in cardiac rehab, this method of performance improvement is often the only one they can cope with, because their ability is so low that necessary loading norms that would be required for endurance training cannot be achieved. Coordination exercises can be varied as desired and adapted to individual limitations. Patients with different levels of ability can train together, and everyone in the group can train successfully.

The Effect of Medication on Heart Rate Behavior

Medication is standard therapy for cardiovascular diseases and supplements exercise. Regular exercise normalizes high blood pressure, making it possible to stop taking medication. However, it is well-known that, in practice, hardly any patients can manage without medication. That is why the limiting or activating effect of the drugs concerned must be known. Exercise increases the metabolism, raises body temperature and changes blood volume distribution, all of which can affect the way the medication works.

Conversely, medication can affect biological parameters that characterize the physiological state during exercise. The best-known example of this is the effect of medication on the heart rate as a parameter for evaluating the demand on the cardiovascular system. Beta blocker therapy reduces the heart rate by at least 10 bpm [63], and the frequency of taking the medicine must be taken into account. The longer the time between when the medication is taken and when training takes place, the lower the effect on the heart rate. Heart rate tachograms show recordings that illustrate the effect of beta blocker therapy on heart rate behavior.

The HR tachogram (fig. 3/6.5) shows the heart rate behavior of a healthy individual age 55 who fulfils all the criteria for health according to medical standards. The heart rate increase at the start of the workout and drop at the end of the workout can be clearly seen.

The fatigue-induced drop in heart rate at the end of the workout does not return it to the starting level. Compared to this, the heart rate tachogram of the cardiac patient is not dynamic at all (fig. 4/6.5). The beginning and end of the workout cannot be discerned from the heart rate curve.

Drugs like calcium antagonists, ACE inhibitors, nitrates, cardiac glycerides, anticoagulants and diuretics are also used in medication therapy, which affect the working tolerance and the biological parameters in different ways. Taking calcium antagonists will not affect the physical performance. The heart rate when taking some medications can be reduced by between 10-15 bpm due to the inhibiting effect on the sinoatrial node. ACE inhibitors improve working tolerance and do not lead to changes in measurable parameters. Likewise, taking cardiac glycerides has a beneficial effect on working tolerance.

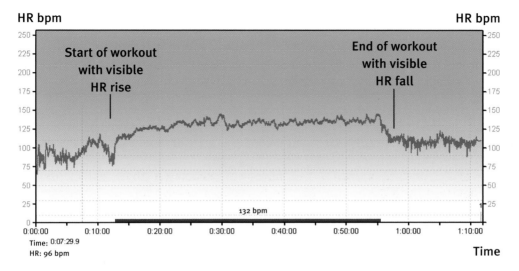

Fig. 3/6.5: Heart rate tachogram of a healthy 55-year-old man who does not take beta blockers during a walking workout

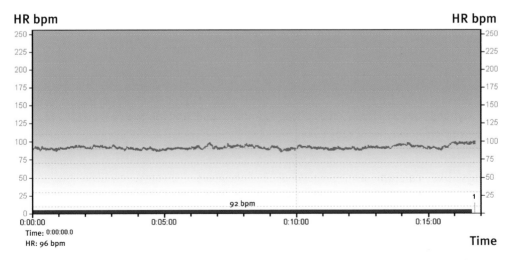

Fig: 4/6.5: Heart rate tachogram of a 58-year-old cardiac patient undergoing beta blocker therapy during a walking workout

TRAINING FOR DIFFERENT TARGET GROUPS

Training with Heart Failure and Coronary Heart Disease

About 1% of the total population suffers from chronic heart failure [14]. This particularly concerns people over 50. The average "five-year survival" of patients following diagnosis applies to about 50%. This makes chronic heart failure the most frequent cause of death in our society [5].

Heart failure means a cardiac weakness (inefficient pumping), when the heart is no longer able to pump sufficient blood around the body in order to supply the organs with blood either at rest or under loading [17].

The heart failure patient suffers, depending on the stage of the disease (NYHA I – IV), from shortness of breath, general muscle weakness and being easily fatigued. The combination of these symptoms results in a generally reduced performance level for the patient. The etiology of heart failure is varied.

The most frequent causes are ischemic heart disease (60-80%), chronic high blood pressure (10-20%) and heart valve disease (5-10%). In the prevention and rehabilitation of heart failure patients, exercise has established itself as a recognized form of therapy.

Contrary to former assumptions, that patients with greatly reduced left ventricular function and NYHA stage IV should be excluded from therapeutic exercise, Niebauer et al. [44], have shown that patients with pronounced load intolerance (NYHA III-IV) derive particular benefit from exercise.

From this point of view, LVEF% and NYHA are not required to control training and do not necessarily reveal anything about the physical performance level. The VO_2max and heart rate reserve (see chapter 2.4) are much more important criteria for physical ability and trainability.

That is why it is recommended to base sport and exercise therapy on the WEBER classification and AHA guidelines (cf. table 1/6.5). Using these criteria, after an initial diagnosis, patients can be classified into risk groups A to E. The risk groups differ in VO_2max, metabolic equivalent, maximal power (watt/kg) and VO_2 at the anaerobic threshold (AT).

Tab. 1/6.5:
Classification of loading limits of patients with heart failure according to the WEBER classification [62] and AHA guidelines [3].

Risk Class	Difficulty	VO$_2$max (ml/kg/min)	MET	Power (Watt/kg)	AT (ml/kg/min)
A	Light to none	> 20	> 5.7	> 1.5	> 14
B	Light to moderate	16 – 20	4.5 – 5.7	1.0 – 1.5	11 – 14
C	Moderate to hard	10 – 16	2.8 – 4.5	0.5 – 1.0	8 – 11
D	Hard	6 – 10	1.7 – 2.8	< 0.5	5 – 8
E	Very hard	< 0.5	< 1.7	< 0.5	< 4

Training with High Blood Pressure

According to international classification, there are three degrees of hypertension. Exercise does not need to be restricted in the case of the first two: mild (syst. 140-159/diast. 90-99) and moderate (syst. 160-179/diast. 100-109) [31], as it does not cause high cardiovascular pressure. However, in the case of severe hypertension (syst > 180, diast. > 110), exercise must be restricted. Sports that involve static loads should be avoided, dynamic and endurance sports are suitable for sufferers of hypertension. Care should be taken that the blood pressure only rises moderately and slowly during exercise. The higher the rise in blood pressure during exercise, the greater the risk [49]!

Training with Heart Rhythm Disturbance

Heart rhythm disturbances are non-specific and often occur as secondary symptoms of other illnesses. Unmonitored and inadequately treated heart rhythm disturbances are contraindications for sports and exercise therapy [49]. Exercise intensity depends on the appearance of complications during the initial performance diagnostic check-up.

The exercise heart rate should be 10-15 bpm below the symptom-limiting value that showed up in the stress ECG. The heart rate tachogram of a 57-year-old patient with absolute arrhythmia illustrates that heart rate disturbance can mean that exercise cannot be controlled by heart rate. The tachogram cannot be interpreted and is unsuitable for use in exercise management.

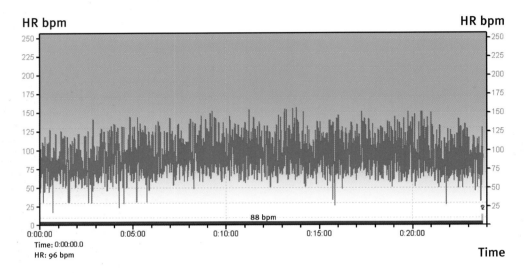

Fig. 5/6.5: Walking – a patient with absolute arrhythmia

7 FREQUENTLY ASKED QUESTIONS (FAQ)

Does a Transmitter Belt always Have to Be Worn?

A continuous and ECG accurate measurement can only be provided/guaranteed by a transmitter belt worn around the chest. There can be significant differences between the pulse measurement on the wrist and the heart rate measurement during exercise. The heart rate measurement corresponds to the number of heart beats per minute.

The pulse corresponds to the mechanical pulse of the blood as it flows through the blood vessels. The traditional method of taking the pulse from the one of the big arteries, e.g., the carotid artery, is practically impossible while training. After training it is affected by a high error rate when counting the beats and by the rapid drop in pulse rate once the load has stopped.

Doesn't the Transmitter Belt Restrict Breathing?

If the transmitter is not fastened too tightly under the chest, it will not restrict breathing. The new textile transmitter Polar WearLink® feels better when you wear it, as only the small transmitter unit is made of rigid material, the rest of the transmitter is made of a strip of fabric into which electrodes are woven.

How do I, as a Beginner, Manage to Use All the Functions of the Wrist Unit?

Every monitor comes with a thorough and user-friendly manual that explains all the functions. The heart rate monitor is also operated by a menu system, similar to that which you would use on a computer or cell phone. The functions are tailored to you, so that their use is self-explanatory.

Why do I Need to Use a Heart Rate Monitor?

This is needed to ensure that you are training at the right intensity and to be able to measure the intensity during the workout. The heart rate is the most reliable and accurate indicator for load intensity. Furthermore, heart rate measurement can help you to increase your awareness of your own body, so that you can evaluate load intensity better yourself. Quite simply, it helps you to get to know your body better.

How Long Do Heart Rate Monitor Batteries Last?

They last for 2-3 years for recreational users with average frequent use and appropriate maintenance.

What Should Senior Athletes, Athletes with Previous Illnesses, or Those Who Take Regular Medication Be Careful of?

For athletes with previous illnesses (e.g., after a heart attack) or who take regular medication (e.g., beta blockers for high blood pressure), it is very important to monitor the load intensity in order to avoid the risk of physical over-exertion.

These users should not be guided by the OwnZone® or OwnIndex®, as these functions are based on heart rate and heart rate variability. When these parameters are altered by medication or illness, they can no longer give accurate information about the state of the body during exercise or during daily life.

For optimal and healthy training, current advice from your physician regarding heart rate is required. This can also be obtained in centers that offer performance diagnoses (a doctor should be present).

Using the performance diagnosis, the doctor or sports therapist can see the current performance level and how the heart rate and blood pressure behave during exercise. From these tests, the experienced doctor/therapist can determine heart rate limits for healthy and effective training for patients. These values can be stored in the heart rate monitor. These tests should be repeated at regular intervals (see chapter 6.4).

Can One Workout with a Heart Rate Monitor if One Has Had a Pacemaker Fitted?

The expert opinion of the heart pacemaker institute in Germany made the following statement about the influence of implanted pacemakers by POLAR heart rate monitors:

That the induced voltage of less than 1mV for all known heart pacemakers is well below the impact threshold of 5 kHz. Any impact or danger for patients with implanted heart pacemakers due to wearing a POLAR heart rate monitor can be ruled out.

However, all heart pacemaker wearers should see their doctor before using a POLAR heart rate monitor.

KEYWORD INDEX

BIBLIOGRAPHY

[1]   Achten, J. (2002). *Influence of exercise intensity and training on substrate utilization. A thesis to the School of Sport and Exercise Sciences.* University of Birmingham.

[2]   Akalan, C., Kravitz, L. & Robergs, R. A. (2004, Mai/Juni). VO_2max: Essentials of the most widely used test in Exercise Physiology. *ACSM Health and Fitness Journal*, 5-9.

[3]   American Heart Association (2000). Assessment of Functional Capacity in Clinical and Research Applications. *Circulation*, 102, 1591-1597.

[4]   American Heart Association (2003). Exercise and Heart Failure. *Circulation*, 107, 1210-1225.

[5]   Anker, S., Werdan, K. & Rüter, F. (2003). Der Patient mit chronischer Herzinsuffizienz. In K. Werdan, H.-J. Trappe & H.-R. Zerkowski (Hrsg.), *Das Herzbuch – praktische Herz-Kreislauf-Medizin* (S. 594-650). München: Urban & Fischer.

[6]   Åstrand, P.-O. & Rodahl, E. K. (1970). *Textbook of Work Physiology*. New York: Mc Graw-Hill.

[7]   Belardinelli, R., Georgiou, D. & Scocco, V. (1995). Low intensity exercise training on exercise capacity and gas exchange in patients with chronic heart failure. *J Am Coll Cardiol*, 26, 975-982.

[8]   Benner, K.-U. (1996). *Der Körper des Menschen.* Augsburg: Weltbild Verlag.

[9]   Bjarnason-Wehrens, B., Mayer-Berger, W., Meister, E. R., Baum, K., Hambrecht, R. & Gielen, S. (2004). Einsatz von Kraftausdauertraining und Muskelaufbautraining in der kardiologischen Rehabilitation – Empfehlungen der Deutschen Gesellschaft für Prävention und Rehabilitation von Herz-Kreislauferkrankungen e. V. *Zeitschrift für Kardiologie*, 93, 357-370.

[10]   Borodulin, K., Lakka, T., Laatikainen, T., Laukkanen, R., Kinnunen, H. & Jousilahti, P. (2004). Associations of self-rated fitness and different types of leisure time physical activity with predicted aerobic fitness in 5.346 Finnish adults. *Journal of Physical Activity and Health*, 1, 142-153.

[11]   Bouchard, C. & Rankinen, T. (2001). Individual differences in response to regular physical activity. *Med. Sci. Sports Exerc.*, 6, 446-451.

[12]   Brusis, O. A., Matlik, M. & Unverdorben, M. (2005). *Handbuch der Herzgruppenbetreuung*. Balingen: Spitta Verlag.

[13]   Church, T. S., Earnest, C. P. & Morss, G. M. (2002, September). Field testing of physiological responses associated with Nordic Walking. *Research quarterly for exercise and sport*, 73, 296-300.

[14]   Cowie, M. R., Mosterd, A. A., Wood, D. A., Deckers, J. W., Poole-Wilson, P. A., Sutton, G. C. & Grobbee, D. E. (1997). The epidemiology of heart failure. *Eur Heart J*, 18, 208-225.

[15] Demopoulos, L., Bijou, R. & Fergus, I. (1997). Exercise training in patients with severe congestive heart failure: Enhancing peak aerobic capacity while minimizing the increase in ventricular wall stress. *J Am Coll Cardiol*, 29, 597-603.

[16] Denk, H., Pache, D. & Schaller, H.-J. (2003). *Handbuch Alterssport*. Schorndorf: Hofmann Verlag.

[17] Erdmann, E. (2003). *Herzinsuffizienz – Ursachen, Pathophysiologie und Therapie*. Stuttgart: Wissenschaftliche Verlagsgesellschaft.

[18] European society of Cardiology (2000). Recommentions for exercise training in chronic heart failure patients. *European Heart Journal*, 22, 125-135.

[19] Gielen, S. & Hambrecht, R. (2003). Chronische Herzinsuffizienz: Schonung oder Training? *Cardiovasc*, 2, 22-26.

[20] Güth, V. & Schröter, J. (1998). Die beim Gehen auftretenden Momente und Kräfte. In J. Wiemeyer (Hrsg.), *Der Gang des Menschen – multidisziplinär betrachtet* (S. 14-18). Schriftenreihe des Instituts für Sportwissenschaft der Technischen Universität Darmstadt.

[21] Hautala, A. J., Mäkikallio, T. H., Kiviniemi, A., Laukkanen, R. T., Nissilä, S., Huikuri H. V. & Tulppo, M. P. (2003). Cardiovascular autonomic function correlates with the response to aerobic training in healthy sedentari subjects. *Am J Physiol Heart Circ Physiol*, 285, H1747-H1752.

[22] Hoff, P., Jaenicke, J. & Miram, W. (1985). *Biologie heute* 2 G. Hannover: Schrödel Verlag.

[23] Hollmann, W. & Hettinger, T. (2000). *Sportmedizin – Grundlagen für Arbeit, Training und Präventivmedizin*. Stuttgart: Schattauer Verlag.

[24] Hottenrott, K. & Zülch, M. (2004). *Ausdauertrainer Radsport*. Reinbek: Rowohlt.

[25] Hottenrott, K. & Zülch, M. (2004). *Ausdauertraining, Fitness und Gesundheit*. Reinbek: Rowohlt.

[26] Hottenrott, K. & Urban, V. (2004). *Das große Buch vom Skilanglauf*. Aachen: Meyer & Meyer.

[27] Hottenrott, K. & Zülch, M. (2003). *Ausdauertrainer Laufen*. Reinbek: Rowohlt.

[28] Hottenrott, K., Lauenroth, A. & Schwesig, R. (2004). Einfluss eines 8wöchigen Walkingtrainings auf die HRV bei über 60jährigen. In K. Hottenrott (Hrsg.), *Herzfrequenzvariabilität im Fitness- und Gesundheitssport* (S. 191-197). Hamburg: Czwalina.

[29] Hottenrott, K. (2002). Grundlagen zur Herzfrequenzvariabilität und Anwendungsmöglichkeiten im Sport. In Hottenrott, K. (Hrsg.), *Herzfrequenzvariabilität im Sport – Prävention, Rehabilitation und Training* (S. 9-26). Hamburg: Czwalina.

[30] Hottenrott, K. & Vestweber, K. (2002). Einfluss einer speziellen Entspannungs- und Konzentrationstechnik (Freeze-Frame®) auf Parameter der Herzfrequenz-variabilität. In K. Hottenrott (Hrsg.), *Herzfrequenzvariabilität im Sport – Prävention, Rehabilitation und Training* (S. 141-156). Hamburg: Czwalina.

[31]   Kaplan, N. M., Deveraux, R. B. & Miller, H. S. (1994). Systemic hypertension. *Med Sci Sports Exerc*, 26, 268-270.

[32]   Laukkanen, R. & Hynninen, E. (eds.) (1997). *Guide for the UKK Institute 2-km Walking Test*. UKK Institute, 5th rev. ed., Tampere.

[33]   Laukkanen, R., Kukkonen-Harjula, K., Oja, P., Rasanen, M. & Vuori, I. (2000) Prediction of change in maximal aerobic power by the 2-km Walk Test after walking training in middle-aged adults. *Int J Sports Med*, 20, 113-116.

[34]   Laukkanen, R. (2005). *Inhalte und Prinzipien des Keeps U Fit Own Trainings-Programms in Polar Herzfrequenz-Messgeräten*. Unveröff. Manuskript.

[35]   Leon, A. S., Casal, D. & Jacobs, D.R. Jr. (1996). Effects of 2000 kcal per week of walking and stair climbing on physical fitness and risk factors for coronary heart disease. *Journal of Cardiopoulmonary Rehabilitation*, 16, 183-192.

[36]   Lipponen, S., Mäkikallio, T., Tulppo, M. & Röning, J. (1998, März). *Finding Structure in Fitness Data. Proceedings of the Second International Conference on the Practical Application of Knowledge Discovery and Data Mining (PADD98) in London*, UK, pp. 101-109.

[37]   Lipponen, S., Väinämö, K., Mäkikallio, T., Tulppo, M. & Röning, J. (1997, Mai). *Approximating Aerobic Fitness With Neural Networks Applying PCA, Proceedings of 1997*. Finnish Signal Processing Symposium (Finsig'97), Tampere University of Technology, Pori School of Technology and Economics, Pori, Finnland, pp. 158-162.

[38]   Meyer, K. & Foster, C. (2003). Muskelaufbau im Zentrum des kardiovaskulären Trainings. *Dt. Zeitschrift für Sportmedizin*, 55, 70-74.

[39]   Meyer, K. (2000). Neue Aspekte zum körperlichen Training bei chronischen Herzinsuffizienz. *Deutsche Zeitschrift für Sportmedizin*, 51 (9), 286-289.

[40]   Mosterd, A. (1998). Epidemiology of Heart failure: contours of an impending epidemic?. *Netherlands J of Med.*, 53, 235-244.

[41]   Mück-Weymann, M. (2004). Anwendung der Herzfrequenzvariabilitätsmessung in Medizin und Psychologie. In K. Hottenrott (Hrsg.), *Herzfrequenzvariabilität im Fitness- und Gesundheitssport* (S. 55-64). Hamburg: Czwalina

[42]   Neumann, G., Pfützner, A. & Hottenrott, K. (2000). *Alles unter Kontrolle: Ausdauersport*. Aachen: Meyer & Meyer.

[43]   Neumann, G. & Hottenrott, K. (2002). *Das große Buch vom Laufen*. Aachen: Meyer & Meyer.

[44]   Niebauer, J., Hambrecht, R., Marburger, C., Hauer, K., Velich, T., von Hodenberg, E. & Schlierf, G., Kubler,W. & Schuler, G. (1995). Impact of intensive physical exercise and low fat diet on collateral vessel formation in stable angina pectoris and angiographically confirmed coronary artery diseas. *Am J Cardiol*, 76, 771-775.

[45]   Penzlin, H. (1996). *Lehrbuch der Tierphysiologie*. Jena: Fischer Verlag.

[46]   Porcari, J. P., Hendrickson, T. L., Walter, P. R., Terry, L. & Walsko, G. (1997). The physiological responses to walking with and without Power Poles on treadmill exercise. *Research Quarterly for exercise and sport*, 68, 161-166.

[47]   Roschinsky, J. (2003). *Fatburning – Workout, Ausdauer, Ernährung*. Aachen: Meyer & Meyer Verlag.

[48]   Rost, R. (2001). *Lehrbuch der Sportmedizin*. Köln: Deutscher Ärzte Verlag.

[49]   Rost, R. (2005). *Sport und Bewegungstherapie bei inneren Erkrankungen*. Köln: Dt. Ärzteverlag.

[50]   Samitz, G. & Mensink, G. (2002). *Körperliche Aktivität in der Prävention und Therapie*. München: Hans Marseille Verlag.

[51]   Schiebel, F., Heitkamp, H.C., Thoma, A., Hipp, A. & Horstmann, T. (2003). Nordic Walking und Walking im Vergleich. *Deutsche Zeitschrift für Sportmedizin*, 54 (7/8), 43.

[52]   Schwarz, M., Schwarz, L., Urhausen, A., Ebersohl, A. & Kindermann, W. (2001). Vergleich des Beanspruchungsprofils beim Walking, Jogging und bei der Fahrradergometrie bei unterschiedlich leistungsfähigen Personen. *Deutsche Zeitschrift für Sportmedizin*, 52 (4), 136.

[53]   Shephard, R. J. & Balady, G. (1999). Exercise as cardiovascular therapy. *Circulation*, 99, 963-972.

[54]   Shvartz, E. & Reibold, R. C. (1990). Aerobic fitness norms for males und females aged 6 to 75 years: a review. *Aviat Space Environ Med,* 61, 3-11.

[55]   Stilgebauer, F., Reißnecker, S. & Steinacker, J. M. (2004). Herzfrequenzvorgaben für Ausdauertraining von Herzpatienten. *Deutsche Zeitschrift für Sportmedizin,* 10, 295-296.

[56]   Stoll, O. & Ziemainz, H. (2002). *Mentale Trainingsformen im Langstreckenlauf.* Butzbach-Griedel: Afra.

[57]   Tamminen, S., Laurinen, P. & Röning, J. (1999, Juni). *Comparing Regression Trees with Neural Networks in Aerobic Fitness Approximation, Proc of International ICSC Symposium on Advances in Intelligent Data Analysis*, in Rochester, New York, USA, pp. 414-419.

[58]   Tourpouzidis, A. (2004). Über die Problematik der Trainingssteuerung in der stationären kardiologischen Rehabilitation. *Bewegungstherapie und Gesundheitssport,* 20, 18-21.

[59]   Väinämö, K., Mäkikallio, T., Tulppo, M. & Röning, J. (1998, Mai): *A Neuro-Fuzzy Approach to Aerobic Fitness Classification: a multistructure solution to the context-sensitive feature selection problem.* Proc. WCCI '98, in Anchorage, Alaska, USA, pp. 797-802

[60]   Väinämö, K., Nissilä, S., Mäkikallio, T. Tulppo, M. & Röning, J. (1996, Juni): *Artificial Neural Networks for Aerobic Fitness Approximation, International Conference on Neural Networks* (ICNN '96), pp. 1939-1944.

[61]   Veltman, J. A. & Gaillard, A.W.K. (1993). Indices of mental workload in a complex task environment. *Neuropsychobiology,* 28, 72-75.

[62]   Weber, K. T., Janicki, J. S. & McElroy, T. P. (1987). Determination of aerobic capacity and the severity of chronic cardiac and circulation failure. *Circulation,* 76 (Suppl VI), VI40–VI45.

[63] Wollring, U. (2005). *Gymnastik im Herz- und Alterssport.* Aachen: Meyer und Meyer Verlag.

[64] www.neuro24.de

[65] www.destatis.de/basis/d/gesu/gesutab8.htm

Photo Credits

Jacket design: Jens Vogelsang, Germany

Jacket photos: Polar Electro Germany

Other photos: adidas
Kristin Ringel
Kuno Hottenrott
Polar Electro Germany
FISCHER GmbH Germany

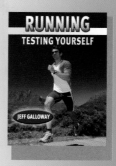

Competence in Triathlon

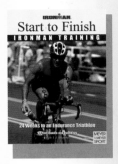

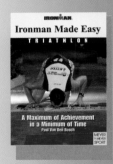
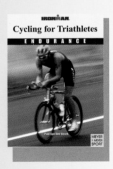
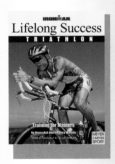